D1545010

I lived in Brooklyn. I'm, say, eight or nine years old. When I come to visit my cousin on 85th Street, Yorkville section, he says to his friends, one by one —
"This is Henry, Henry Miller from Brooklyn." And they almost bow to me, the boys. I'm already made leader of the gang, because I'm from another neighborhood. It's as if I'm from another planet!

This is Henry, Henry Miller from Brooklyn

Conversations with the Author from *The Henry Miller Odyssey*

by Robert Snyder

Nash Publishing, Los Angeles

PS
3525
.I5454
T

Excerpts from *Black Spring, Tropic of Cancer,* and *Tropic of Capricorn* reprinted by permission of Grove Press, Inc., 53 East 11 Street, New York, N.Y. 10003; from *Colossus of Maroussi,* reprinted by permission of New Directions Publishing Corp., USA, and Laurence Pollinger, Ltd., England; excerpts from letters to Lawrence Durrell and Alfred Perlès are reprinted by permission of Curtis Brown, Ltd., in England, and E. P. Dutton & Co., Inc. from *Art and Outrage: A Correspondence about Henry Miller.* Copyright © 1959 by Alfred Perlès and Lawrence Durrell in the United States.
And for permission to quote from his letters and his works, our grateful thanks to Henry Miller.

COPYRIGHT © 1974 BY ROBERT SNYDER

ALL RIGHTS RESERVED. NO PART OF THIS BOOK
MAY BE REPRODUCED IN ANY FORM OR BY ANY MEANS
WITHOUT PERMISSION IN WRITING FROM THE PUBLISHER

LIBRARY OF CONGRESS CATALOG CARD NUMBER: 73-92969
INTERNATIONAL STANDARD BOOK NUMBER: 08402-1076-0

PUBLISHED SIMULTANEOUSLY IN THE UNITED STATES AND CANADA
BY NASH PUBLISHING CORPORATION, 9255 SUNSET BOULEVARD
LOS ANGELES, CALIFORNIA 90069

PRINTED IN THE UNITED STATES OF AMERICA

FIRST PRINTING

*This scrapbook is lovingly dedicated to my wife,
loving, laughing Allegra, who patiently indulged me in
my devotion, even addiction, to the seemingly
endless filming of* Henry Miller *and, now, this
little book; and who affectionately encouraged me,
urging me on to see them through.*

Acknowledgments

Above all the many who helped make this finished book possible, I thank my editor, Ruth Glushanok, whose knowledge of the author, the craft of bookmaking, and sympathy with my trials got me over the hurdles, and the job done; whatever its faults, they are mine.

My heartfelt thanks to Kadi Tint, art director, who applied her extensive knowledge and sensibilities to the actual construction of the book.

To Robert A. Fitzgerald, Jr., who gave me expert assistance in the selection of photographs, and to the photography of documents and memorabilia in the Special Collections Division of the UCLA library; to Brooke Whiting, and the library staff, and, of course, to Lawrence Clark Powell, who was responsible for establishing the Henry Miller Archives at UCLA, my grateful thanks for their continuing assistance to me in getting together the photographs for parts of the book as well as the film.

Credit for all the photos from the film negative is due to Baylis Glascock, director of photography; for the production stills, to Jaime L. Snyder; and for the photos of Henry Miller's Brooklyn, to Edward A. Lazarus.

Chronology

Born in the Yorkville section of Manhattan, New York, New York, December 26, of American parents of German ancestry. Moved to Brooklyn in first year.	*1891*
Lived in the streets of Williamsburg, Brooklyn, known as the 14th Ward.	*1892-1900*
Moved to "the Street of Early Sorrows" (Decatur Street) in the Bushwick section of Brooklyn.	*1901*
Met first love, Cora Seward, at Eastern District High School, Brooklyn.	*1907*
Entered City College of New York and left after two months—rebelled against educational methods. Took job with Atlas Portland Cement Company, financial district, New York. Began period of rigorous athletic discipline that lasted seven years.	*1909*
Began affair with first mistress, Pauline Chouteau of Phoebus, Virginia, a woman old enough to be my mother.	*1910*
Traveled through the West. Worked as ranch hand in effort to break away from city life. Met Emma Goldman, the celebrated anarchist, in San Diego—a turning point in my life.	*1913*
Back in New York, worked with father in his tailor shop; tried to turn business over to the employees. Met Frank Harris, my first contact with a great writer.	*1914*
Married Beatrice Sylvas Wickens of Brooklyn, a pianist.	*1917*
Daughter born, named Barbara Sylvas, now known as Barbara Miller.	*1919*
After working several months as a messenger, became employment manager of the messenger department of Western Union in New York.	*1920*
Wrote first book, *Clipped Wings*, during three weeks' vacation from Western Union duties.	*1922*
Fell in love with June Edith Smith whom I met while she was working in a Broadway dance palace.	*1923*
Left Western Union determined never to take a job again but to devote entire energy to writing. Divorced first wife and married June Smith.	*1924*
Began writing career in earnest, accompanied by great poverty. Sold prose poems, *Mezzotints*, from door to door.	*1925*
Opened a speakeasy in Greenwich Village with wife June. While working in Park Department in Queens, compiled notes for complete autobiographical cycle in 24 hours. Exhibited watercolors in June Mansfield's Roman Tavern, Greenwich Village.	*1927*
Toured Europe for one year with June on money given to her by an admirer.	*1928*
Returned to New York, where the novel *This Gentile World* was completed.	*1929*

1930	Returned to Europe alone, taking the manuscript of another novel which was lost by Edward Titus, editor of *This Quarter,* Paris. Left New York with ten dollars loaned by Emil Schnellock; intended to go to Spain but, after staying in London a while, went to Paris and remained there. Befriended by Richard G. Osborn and Alfred Perlès; I stayed with Osborn during the winter and spring of 1931/32 at Rue Auguste Bartholdi.
1931-32	Met Anaïs Nin, the writer, in Louveciennes. Began writing *Tropic of Cancer* while walking the streets and sleeping wherever possible. Worked as proofreader on the Paris edition of the *Chicago Tribune.* Taught English at Lycée Carnot (Dijon) during the winter.
1933	Took apartment with Alfred Perlès in Clichy and visited Luxembourg with him. The *Black Spring* period; great fertility, great joy. Began book on Lawrence which was never finished. June returned to Europe, but after a brief stay asked for a divorce and left.
1934	Moved to 18 Villa Seurat on the same day that *Tropic of Cancer* was published—a decisive moment. The original manuscript rewritten three times. It was three times as long as the published work. Divorced from June in Mexico City by proxy.
1935	*Aller Retour New York* published in October. Met Conrad Moricand, the astrologer. Began the *Hamlet* correspondence with Michael Fraenkel in November. First edition of *Alf Letter* appeared in September.
1936	Visited New York again—January to April. Practiced psychoanalysis. Began correspondence with Count Keyserling after reading his *Travel Diary. Black Spring* published in June.
1937	Momentous meeting with Lawrence Durrell. *Scenario* published with illustration by Abe Rattner. Began publication of *The Booster* and *Delta* with Alfred Perlès. Went to London during the winter for a few weeks to visit Perlès. Met W. T. Symons, T. S. Eliot and Dylan Thomas.
1938	Began writing for French revue, *Volontés,* in January, the publication month of *Money and How It Gets That Way.* Second edition of *Alf* appeared in June; *Max and the White Phagocytes* published in September.
1939	*Tropic of Capricorn* published in February and the *Hamlet* letters with Michael Fraenkel later in year. Left Villa Seurat in June for sabbatical year's vacation. End of a very important period of close association with Anaïs Nin, Alfred Perlès, Michael Fraenkel, Hans Reichel, Abe Rattner, David Edgar, Conrad Moricand, Georges Pelorson, Henri Fluchère, et al. Toured southern France. Left for Athens on July 14, arriving at Durrell's home in Corfu, Greece, in August. Back and forth to Athens several times, visited some of the islands, toured the Peloponnesus. High-water mark in life's adventures thus far. Met George C. Katsimbalis (the Colossus); George Seferiades, the poet; Ghika, the painter, et al. Found real home, real climate. Source of regular income stopped with death of Paris publisher (Jack Kahane, the Obelisk Press) the day after war was declared.

Returned to New York in February, where I met Sherwood Anderson and John Dos Passos. Stayed with John and Flo Dudley at Caresse Crosby's home in Bowling Green, Virginia, during the summer. Wrote *The Colossus of Maroussi, The World of Sex, Quiet Days in Clichy* and began *The Rosy Crucifixion*. — *1940*

Made tour of U.S.A. accompanied part of the way by Abraham Rattner, the painter, from October 20, 1940, until October 9, 1941. Met Dr. Marion Souchon, Weeks Hall, Swami Prabhavananda, Alfred Stieglitz, Fernand Léger and John Marin. Father died while I was in Mississippi, and I returned to New York. Left for California in June 1942. Continued with *The Rosy Crucifixion* (finished half of it) and with *The Air-Conditioned Nightmare* (finished about two-thirds). — *1941*

Made 200 to 300 watercolors. Exhibited at Beverly Glen (The Green House), American Contemporary Gallery, Hollywood, with success. — *1942*

Exhibited watercolors at Santa Barbara Museum of Art and in London. Seventeen or more titles edited for publication in England and America. Year of fulfillment and realization. First "successful" year from material standpoint in whole life. Was called to Brooklyn in October due to illness of mother. Visited Herbert F. West at Dartmouth College, New Hampshire, and exhibited at Yale. Married Janina M. Lepska in Denver, Colorado, December 18, 1944. Moved to Big Sur, my first real home in America. Emil White arrived in May from Alaska to offer his services. Met Jean Page Wharton, who had a great influence on my thinking. — *1944*

Finished *Sexus* at Keith Evans's cabin, Partington Ridge. Started translation, which was never finished, of *Season in Hell*. Daughter Valentine born November 19. Bezalel Schatz, Israeli painter, arrived December 26 (my birthday). — *1945*

Moved to shack at Anderson Creek in January. Began work on *Into the Night Life* book with Schatz. Also began book about Rimbaud: *The Time of the Assassins*. Met Leon Shamroy, who eventually bought over 30 of my watercolors. Received news from Paris that $40,000 had accumulated to my credit, which I neglected to collect. Jean Wharton offered us her home in Partington Ridge, to pay for whenever we could. — *1946*

Took possession of Wharton's house on Ridge in February. Began writing *Plexus. Into the Night Life* book completed. — *1947*

Wrote *The Smile at the Foot of the Ladder*. Son, Tony, born August 28. — *1948*

Finished *Plexus*. Began writing *The Books in My Life*. — *1949*

Separated from wife, Janina Lepska; the children went to live with her in Los Angeles. Finished *The Books in My life*. — *1951*

Eve McClure arrived April 1 to live with me. Began writing *Nexus*. — *1952*

Divorced from Janina Lepska. Left for tour of Europe with Eve on December 29. Arrived in Paris for New Year's Eve. — *1952*

Big year—best since Clichy. Invited to stay at home of Maurice Nadeau, former editor of *Combat* and chief organizer of the *Defense* — *1953*

of Henry Miller. Visited Rabelais's house outside Chinon, then to Wells, England, to see Perlès and wife. Took in Shakespeare's house at Stratford-on-Avon with Schatzes. Flying visit to John Cowper Powys in Corwyn, Wales. Back to Paris. Returned to Big Sur at the end of August. Married Eve McClure in Carmel Highlands, *chez* Ephraim Doner, in December.

1954 Alfred Perlès arrived in November to write *My Friend Henry Miller.* Traveling exhibition of watercolors in Japan. Began writing *Big Sur and the Oranges of Hieronymus Bosch.*

1955 Barbara Sandford, daughter by first marriage, came to see me; hadn't seen her since 1925. Perlès left for London in May. Had visit from Buddhadeva Bose of Calcutta, Bengali poet. Wrote *Reunion in Barcelona.*

1956 Left for Brooklyn in January with Eve to take care of my mother, who was dying. While there, met Ben Grauer of NBC and made recording, *Henry Miller Recalls and Reflects.* Returned to Big Sur. Collection of short pieces translated and published in Hebrew— *Hatzoth Vahetzi* ("Half Past Midnight"). Finished *Big Sur and the Oranges of Hieronymus Bosch* book.

1957 Rewrote *Quiet Days in Clichy* upon recovery of manuscript, which had been lost for 15 years. Exhibition of watercolors at Gallery One, London. Completely rewrote *The World of Sex* for publication by Olympia Press, Paris. Exhibition of watercolors in Jerusalem and Tel Aviv. Began writing *Lime Twigs and Treachery* but abandoned it to resume work on *Nexus.* Elected member of National Institute of Arts and Sciences.

1958 Continued work on *Nexus.*

1959 Finished *Nexus* in early April. Left for Europe with Eve and children on April 14. Rented studio on Rue Campagne-Première, Paris, for two months. Visited Danish publisher on trip to Copenhagen with children; Gerald Robitaille acted as "governess." First meeting with Antonio Bibalo, composer of opera *The Smile at the Foot of the Ladder.* Returned to Big Sur in the middle of August. Wrote the three letters contained in *Art and Outrage* (Perlès-Durrell).

1960 Wrote *To Paint Is to Love Again.* Left for Europe April 4 to attend Cannes Film Festival as one of the judges. Spent a few days in Paris, then to Hamburg to visit Ledig-Rowohlt in Reinbek. There met Renate Gerhardt for the first time. After traveling in France and Italy, returned to Big Sur. Returned again to Europe. At Rowohlt Verlag, Reinbek, wrote preface to new edition of Élie Faure's *History of Art* (Gallimard) and several minor pieces, including one in (crazy) German called *Ein Ungebumbelte Füchselbiss* for a little revue called *Rhinozeros.* Also did drawings and watercolors for editor of the revue, Rudolf Dienst. Made a number of watercolors and played much Ping-Pong at Rowohlt Verlag. With Ledig and others, visited Mölln (Til Eulenspiegel's birthplace) and the Luneberg Heide, Bremen and other places. Over Christmas holidays wrote first draft of *Just Wild About Harry, chez* Renate Gerhardt.

1961 Toured Germany, Austria, Switzerland, Italy, Portugal and Spain.

Visited Marino Marini, the famous sculptor, who did my head in bronze. Returned to Pacific Palisades from London in November. In this year Grove Press published *Tropic of Cancer*.

Trip to London to visit Perlès and made tape with him for C.B.C. (television). Visited Ireland with him and his wife for a month. Then on to Paris to visit old and new friends. Went to Berlin, where I made ten copper-plate etchings and more watercolors at home of Renate Gerhardt. Returned to New York at end of May. Received final decree of divorce from Eve in June. Back to Pacific Palisades in July. Left for Edinburgh middle of July to attend Writers' Conference. Met Durrell there and his friend Dr. Raymond Mills. Made tape with Durrell for BBC Radio, Geoffrey Bridson interviewing. Left with Durrell for Paris, where we made readings for recordings from our books (for La Voix de l'Auteur). The two *Tropics* were published in Italian (from Switzerland) and *Cancer* in Finnish; immediately suppressed. Also *Cancer* in Hebrew, in two thin paperback volumes. *Capricorn* published by Grove Press. Returned to Pacific Palisades end of November. *1962*

Cancer published in England by John Calder—great success. Wrote five or six prefaces for other authors' books: Jack Bilbo, H. E. Bates, George Dibbern, and so on. Also text for Anne Poor's drawings of *Greece*, published by Viking Press. *Capricorn* issued in paperback by Grove Press and *A Private Correspondence*, with Lawrence Durrell (Dutton), and *Black Spring* (Grove Press). Began making silk screens with nuns at Immaculate Heart College, Hollywood. Made 115 watercolors from March to end of July. Moved to Ocampo Drive in Pacific Palisades in February. Contracted for film of *Tropic of Cancer* with Joe Levine. *Just Wild About Harry* published by New Directions, New York. *1963*

Henry Miller on Writing published by New Directions, New York. Watercolor exhibition at Westwood Art Association, Los Angeles. Death of Eve, my fourth wife. Production of the opera *The Smile at the Foot of the Ladder* in Hamburg, Germany, in April. Great success. *Selected Prose* published by MacGibbon and Kee (two volumes), London. *Letters to Anaïs Nin* published by G. P. Putnam's Sons, New York. *1964*
1965

Order and Chaos Chez Hans Reichel published by Loujon Press, Las Vegas, Nevada. *1966*

The opera *The Smile at the Foot of the Ladder* produced in Marseilles, France, in French. *The Henry Miller Odyssey* film begun by Robert Snyder. Began study of Japanese with Michiyo Watanabe. Married Hoki Tokuda on September 10 in Beverly Hills. Honeymoon trip to Paris in September with Hoki. Watercolor show at Daniel Gervis Gallery in Paris. Returned from Europe to Pacific Palisades. Watercolor show in Uppsala, Sweden. Opera *The Smile at the Foot of the Ladder* produced in Trieste, Italy, in Italian, in December. *1967*

Lawrence Durrell visited me in Pacific Palisades in March. Water- *1968*

color show toured Japan. *Collector's Quest*, a correspondence with J. Rives Childs, published by University Press of Virginia. Began *My Life and Times* with Bradley Smith. New edition of *To Paint Is to Love Again* published by Grossman, New York. This edition includes *Semblance of a Devoted Past*.

1969 Premiere of *The Henry Miller Odyssey* at Royce Hall, UCLA. Took trip to Europe in June to observe progress on *Tropic of Cancer* film. Bob Snyder's one hour TV special, "Henry Miller: Reflections on Writing," shown on NET Festival.

1970 *Tropic of Cancer* film opened in U.S. *Quiet Days in Clichy* film opened in U.S. Two colored lithographs of my watercolors printed and distributed by First Impressions, San Francisco. Three colored lithographs of my watercolors printed and distributed by S. Kubo, Japan. *Insomnia or the Devil at Large* published by Loujon Press, Las Vegas, Nevada. *Entretiens de Paris*, with Georges Belmont (radio and television interviews), published in Paris. Received Book of Year Award in Naples for *Come il Colibri* (*Stand Still Like the Hummingbird*). First and only prize I ever received for my literary work.

1971 *Just Wild About Harry* to be produced in Paris. Publication of *My Life and Times* by Playboy Press. *Smile at the Foot of the Ladder*, special Hallmark edition. "In Honor of Henry Miller's 80th Birthday" celebrations at UCLA with films and exhibits, talks by Larry Powell and Larry Durrell who came over for the event; concurrently celebrated by the American embassy's *Centre Culturel Américain* in Paris (both arranged by Bob Snyder).

1972 *Reflections on the Death of Mishima* and *On Turning Eighty* published by Capra Press; *Henry Miller in Conversation* originally in French, published by Quandrangle Press.

1973 *The Waters Reglitterized* and *First Impressions of Greece*—Capra Press. Larry Durrell here for Mme. Arnaud's film *Poète Maudit* made for European Broadcasting Union. Opera version of *Smile at the Foot of the Ladder* presented in Nice. Two operations in the Fall of 1973. Tom Schiller's short film *Henry Miller Asleep and Awake*. Tony Miller forms Henry Miller Enterprises to reprint limited editions of graphics and art texts.

1974 Larry Durrell here again while Visiting Professor at Cal Tech. Miller made Grand Chevalier, Légion d'Honneur—French Legion of Honor. Valentine Miller founds Sur Valentine Productions to issue limited editions of Henry Miller art.

Prologue

"To write the life of him, who excelled all mankind in writing the lives of others," commences James Boswell in *The Life of Samuel Johnson*, ". . . is an arduous, and may be reckoned in me a presumptuous task." To film the "life" of Henry Miller, all of whose own writing was principally autobiographical, may equally be termed arduous and, perhaps, futile. If it's all in his books, then why a biographical film and, now, another book? The value of the film is clear enough: to have it "live" from the horse's mouth (ah, if we could only see and hear Rousseau or St. Augustine, or other "confessional" writers, unfolding their stories), a living record with facial expressions and body gestures, and with cadence, rhythm, and timbre—even stammers and pauses—of voice that the written word cannot capture. And, of course, "recollected in tranquillity," at a much later remove, remembered . . . misremembered . . . but in any case, fleshing out, supplementing and adding other dimensions to the writings.

But this book—well, it's not a book "in the ordinary sense of the word," . . . it's not "a spit in the eye" as Henry disclaims in *Tropic of Cancer*, nor is it, alas, "a kick in the pants of God, Man, Destiny, Time, Love, Beauty. . . ." It's a transmutation, a reduction of the hours and hours of film and tape that I started to record in 1968, and that has so far yielded *The Henry Miller Odyssey*, a ninety-minute biographical documentary that premiered at UCLA's Royce Hall—covering the Brooklyn years and Paris, with a look into the present; *Reflections on Writing*, a "literary biography"; and an hour's videotape, *Henry Miller Reads and Muses*. And in the reductive process, the lifelike images—reality at 24 frames per second—are frozen into stills, and the living sound into the printed word.

Worse yet, transcription of the oral word in no way equals "writing." I was faced with the problem of translating the transcript of the film's sound track into words on a written page. It would not be *his* writing, of course; Miller is very much a word man—a writer's writer. Rather than seem to be equating this soundtrack of conversations with Miller's often marvelous prose, I chose not to tamper with the words he spoke, but to leave the text with its mm's, hmm's, all the y'knows and don'cha knows, dangling participles and hanging phrases and incomplete sentences.

So this book is only a skimming of the film of the man; and even if there were ten more films, they couldn't be more than an invitation to the man's work, for as he himself has written:

I am neither a scholar nor a critic. My knowledge of Miller's writing was minimal, and I was taking the responsibility for putting this film together. Approaching the deadline, I read more and more feverishly. He saw me hunting through the books in his library; when I told him I was catching up on the Miller canon, he said, "Oh, you don't have to read that stuff; you've got it in your nose."

"My book is the man that I am; the confused man, the negligent man, the lusty, obscene, boisterous, thoughtful, scrupulous, lying diabolically truthful man that I am. . . ."

(and for God's sake, start with *Black Spring* and go all the way through the *Books in My Life* and even beyond). Maurice Wiggin, the television reviewer for the London *Times*, wrote, after having seen some twenty-four minutes of "fragments of an interrupted conversation with the American author" on the BBC:

"Finally there was Henry Miller talking to Robert Snyder. Never seen him before; never read a word he wrote. One of the many gaps in my education. It must be filled! Such candor, such a flow of unaffected, dry crackling candor. Looking like an emaciated, leathery lizard, the old man seemd to have no stances, no consciousness whatever of "image," no opaque film hanging between himself and us. Rare, the rarest thing. He was as free and easy as a dog. . . . If he writes like he talks, he must be wonderfully readable, whether he is a wicked old sinner or not. There's only one way to find out."

And in his yearly roundup, the only program he found memorable and singled out for mention was the Miller program: "Electrified by Henry Miller's appearance on the box, I went out and bought all his books and read them for the first time—I shall never be the same again!"

How did the film come to pass in the first place? How did this "legend in his own time" who had nakedly and mercilessly written his private life and made it public, but who, in fact, insists on and jealously guards his privacy, resisting public appearances and the prying of interviewers, film and TV, ever let me have access to him?

It started one day at a Little League game in Pacific Palisades when my wife and I spotted this wiry, bespectacled, jauntily capped man with his "vélo," watching the game, and recognized him as none other. The Colossus of Big Sur was living in this bourgeois village of Pacific Palisades? Most improbable; surely, only visiting.

But now I became aware that from time to time—at the post office, in and around the town—I was seeing him. And, of course, I asked around; and it was so. He was living here, not five minutes from where we lived. I would find myself following him, at a decent distance, from a car or walking, when I chanced to spot him, never daring to approach him. In the following year, I had occasion to make a short documentary film of Caresse Crosby in her *citta del mondo* in the castle and principality of Roccasinibalda, Italy, "revisiting" the artists and writers of those Passionate Years in Paris between the two great wars—D. H. Lawrence, Ezra Pound, Salvadore Dali, Max Ernst,

with Bob Snyder, examining
stills for *Street of Early Sorrows*.

Anaïs, Ernest Hemingway, René Crevel—and, of course, Henry Miller.

She recalled: "Henry first came to my Black Sun Press in Paris when he was very hard up and very anxious to publish, and he brought me the manuscript of *The Tropic of Cancer*. I read it, and I was horrified; I wouldn't think of publishing it. But I wouldn't publish it now, either. I still think he has written things that are more valuable and more to my taste and beliefs."

But, he's a neighbor of ours; wouldn't it be wonderful to do a film of him? She'd write an introduction to him and ask me personally to convey her regards.

When I returned home, I began to try to reach him. I wrote, and he replied: He wanted to know what was happening to the catalog of artists and writers of the period that Caresse was assembling; and *he didn't want to be filmed!* Once I'd made contact with him, I wrote every six months or so over the next couple of years: Wouldn't he like to see the now finished film of Caresse? No, thanks. He was not to be inveigled into any contact that might betray his self-discipline. (I later discovered that he finds it difficult to say no, just as Larry Durrell recounted, when in response to his first fan letter to *cher maitre* in Paris from Corfu, where Durrell had picked up a copy of *Tropic of Cancer* abandoned in a public toilet, he was surprised to get a response from Miller. Henry generally replies to his mail, especially if the letter has a foreign stamp on it.)

A few years passed in this way, and then I learned from a mutual friend that Pablo Casals was one of his heroes.

Marvelous! I had made the first film of Casals, in which he recorded a master performance of a complete Bach *Suite for Unaccompanied Cello*. Casals' bow would storm the citadel: Would Miller like to have Casals play for him right in his living room? He was suckered.

And so it happened that I went over one evening with my 16mm projector and screen, and ran the film for him. He was most pleased; do I have anything else? I came armed with an experimental filmed magazine-on-the-arts (*Sketchbook 1: Three Americans*) and ran the half hour comprising vignettes of Buckminster Fuller, Igor Stravinsky, and Willem de Kooning. When the light went on he looked at me, saying, "Young man, you've got your life's work cut out for you, haven't you?" I nodded, "Yes, and you're next!"

He laughed, a remarkably throaty chuckle. Was this warm, gentle man the "high priest of obscenity?" A paradox, a paradox. For all the years that ensued of living with him on quite close, even intimate, terms, I can add very little to what he himself revealed: that he, like one

David Frost, by a confirmed appointment, sent a television crew from London to Paris for an interview with Miller—only to find him "indisposed" at the appointed time.

A short film based on Henry's book To Paint is to Love Again.

of his favorite authors, Walt Whitman, is full of contradictions; infinite, he contains opposites. As I once lamented with a would-be interviewer whom he had stood up—the only predictable thing about him is his unpredictability.

After we wrapped up, he invited me to have a drink and asked whether I played Ping-Pong. I hadn't played for years, but having once been a pretty fair athlete, I picked up on it—and was trounced by this seventy-five-year-old who walked with a cane (because of arthritis in his right hip); and I didn't give him the game, either. I was invited back and we talked about the prospects of doing a film. I had explored the financial possibilities, but there wasn't any money, in Hollywood at any rate, for this kind of thing. We agreed to go forward on our own and, prudently, limit ourselves to an art short.

I remember walking out of the house with his "boon companion" Joe Gray, a younger Brooklyn boy, ex-pug, movie extra, and Dean Martin stand-in—Henry's California equivalent of Alf Perlès). And Joe looked at me evenly and said that I seemed to have won the old man's confidence. "I hope you realize that you're starting a five-year project." It seemed absurd. Little did I know how accurate Joe's prediction would prove to be.

We started officially, when some colleagues at the BBC to whom I had mentioned the possibility of filming Henry, commissioned me to do an interview with him. Now we had to face up squarely to the project. Henry said OK, but only on condition that he was not to know it was happening: no giving directions, no manipulation, no asking questions, no light meters scanning his face, no lights, equipment, cables and crews messing around his house. Impossible ground rules for a technological medium such as sound film. I discussed the matter with my resourceful, brilliant young cameraman, Baylis Glascock, who knew, by now, that what I wanted to capture in these happenings was the "itness," not the "aboutness" of the subject. He shot over my shoulder, under my armpit, in response to head, eye, hand, or body motions. He said it was madness, but let's go.

It was spring 1968. Baylis, young Tom Schiller (an apprentice at the time) and I, with minimal and miniaturized film and sound equipment, arrived at Henry's house. He was in the pool doing his daily therapeutic stint of "walking the bar" hand over hand around the pool, tossing beach balls into floating styrofoam hemispheres, swimming, and floating. He is curious to know each piece of equipment we're using and the reason for every move we make. We're set to roll.

"Henry, water being the element it is, and you floating in it . . . what's your earliest memory?"

And the voice, warm, seductive, gravelly, with the timbre of Humphrey Bogart's and the accent of Jimmie Gleason, responds. . . .

Henry Miller in the pool.

<u>Legend for Bob Snyder Photos</u>

1. "Street of Early Sorrows" - Lived here from 9 to 25 yrs. of age
2. Grammar School - graduated 1905
3. Scene of funeral parties after burials
4. Home of first love - walked to + from here from Decatur St. nightly
5. Burlesque house mentioned in "Black Spring"
6. Taken here as child for using bad language
7. Received gilt-edged New Testament for memorizing 23rd Psalm — saw first motion picture here (1898) — Chinaman walking across B'klyn Bridge
8. Trolley passed our home at 662 Driggs Ave.
9. Lugubrious but picturesque street
10. First Grammar School - only stayed here a year or so. (Idol of the teachers)
11. Dirty, big smelly factory - mentioned in "Black Spring"
12. Frequent visitor here. Had first hallucination on "L" station — see books
13. Taken here when very young — to see Lou Hearn and Bonita (by mother)
14. Frequent visitor - see passage on Cleo (belly dancer) in Sexus
15. Favorite street - played here. Like out of fairy tale. Eddie Carney lived here.
16. Wonderful place - X'mas presents - mother making me apologize
17. A ten-20-30 theatre. Corse Payton idol of theatre-goers. Later a crony of father at Wolcott bar
18. Place where bicycle riders met on way to Coney Island
19. Saw old sentimental plays here
20. Where June and I lived after I quit Western Union
21. Favorite library - spent much time here
22. Where June + I lived - wrote first novel here under her name
23. Lived here after return from European trip together (top floor) left here for permanent stay in Europe.
24. Basement - underground life - Jean Kronski living with us. (see Sexus)
25. Visits to good friend Al Burger on this street - wonderful days.
26. Home of Uncle Harry + Aunt Mary - over stable. (see "Black Spring")
27. Interesting street- Daley's fish market, Reynolds Bakery, Vossler's Drug Store, etc.
28. Remembrance of beautiful saloons - meeting father at ferry
29. Beautiful outdoor theatre + beer garden - with mother - beautiful memories
30. Home of the Imhofs - Joey + Tony - like country then! (Later June's place)
31. Scene of family reunions - with Tony + Joey - German-American feasts!
32. One of old-time favorite burlesque houses - formerly Hyde + Beeman's (Kraueemeyer's alley)
33. First Burlesk ever visited - at 15 - with Harry Martin. Fletcher
34. Great joint - dry fucks - Bill Dewar and the nymphomaniacs. Henderson's Band.
35. Upstairs - meet June here as taxi girl (see Sexus)
36. Here I met Cora Seward first love. Eccentric teachers!
37. Enchanting old building, Spanish style - Miss Petty, the Principal!
38. Quit tailor shop for month or two, hoping to become athletic instructor
39. Opposite famous Wolcott Hotel - see "Black Spring"
40. Marvelous memories of rides to Coney Island - also setting pace for famous 6-day Bike Riders!
41. Attended this gym school for several years - 1905-08 probably
42. Joined Boys' Brigade here - "Battery A - Heavy Artillery - rose to a Captain
43. Went often (Sat. nights) with Bob Haase. Always stood up back of orchestra (Saw here Fritz Scheff and other stars from Europe)
44. Went here every Sat. matinee - 10¢ in balcony - my first theatre (vaudeville)
45. Ran this with June in a basement. after customers left - ping pong
46. Probably first exhibition of W.C.'s here - run by wife June (Cellar dive)
47. Frequent visitor - liked atmosphere. Later visited with candies to sell
48. Restaurant where June worked - where she first met Jean Kronski
49. Picturesque quarter - Arabs, Syrians, Spaniards
50. Where I finally quit the Western Union
51. Picturesque old playhouse - saw first good play here - with father
52. Imitation Italian architecture — a landmark
53. Where I walked back + forth on empty stomach many times
54. Picturesque spot - often visited with Emil Schnellock
55. Unforgettable sign - "the smile that won't come off!"

lists, lists, lists: Henry made up lists of places to shoot, in Brooklyn and in Paris, lists of photos, of happenings, of dates.

The Brooklyn Years

Glendale, L. I.,
March 28, 1899

Dear Mamma and Papa,
As it is a dreary rainy
day, so I have plenty
of time to write. We
went to bed last night
at nine o'clock, and we
did not fall to sleep
till half past ten. In
the morning we got up
at seven o'clock, and
after break-fast we went
to Minnie's school.
After school I wrote
this letter. Dear mamma,
Mrs. Imhof would like
to have you to do her
a favor. If the weather
is fine Wednesday, you
should come for dinner
with out fail, if not then
come on Thursday. Mrs.
Imhof would like to
go to the city while
you are here, so some-
body is with Gertrude.
Dear mamma you can
tell Aunt Annie and
Aunt Emily and Grand-
papa, I sent my love on
a long string from
Glendale to 62 Driggs Ave
Brooklyn N. Y. and a
bushel of kisses.
I will close my letter
with best regards to all,
with love and lots of
kisses to you, papa, and
my dear little sister
Lauretta. Hoping you
are all well and happy,
as I am.
I remaine your
loving son,
Henry.

I'd say, my first acquaintance with death—seeing a dead cat in the gutter, I really think so—that was my first big memory; being surprised that the cat was stiff, y'know, and already rotting away. I think that was my first. And then there come a pile of them, like sitting by the window when I'm sick, convalescing, watching the snow fall against the windowpane, the ice form on the window, and tracing patterns on the ice. Sitting by the stove in the kitchen on a very tiny chair and talking to my mother; mostly she was scolding me.

Well . . . I don't have pleasant memories of talks with her.

My mother did the first terrible thing for which I never forgave her, y'know . . . my mother. . . . She says to me, "Henry, I have a wart." I'm only four years old and I'm sitting in this little chair and she says, "Henry, what shall I do with this?" And I say, "Cut it off. With a scissors." Two days later she got blood poisoning and she says, "And you told me to cut it off!" and bang bang bang she slaps me, for telling her to do this. How do you like a mother who'd do that?

Oh, my mother . . . she was a peculiar woman, you know. The neighbors always said she loved me; they said she was very fond of me and all that. I never felt any warmth from her. She never kissed me, never hugged me. I can never remember going to her and putting my arms around her. That was a big loss. I didn't know mothers did that until I visited a friend one day. We're twelve years old and I go home with him; and I hear his mother's voice—they were English—"Jackie, oh Jackie," she says, "darling, how are you? How have you been?" and puts her arms around him. Jesus, I never heard that kind of language; even that tone of voice. . . . Mm. Beautiful.

Because in that stupid German neighborhood they were great disciplinarians. They were brutal people. All my friends, when I'd go home with them they'd say, "Help me, defend me; if my father starts to hit me grab something and let's run!" It was all brutality, discipline. Crazy.

That was the "street of early sorrows" as I call it. Before that was the good time of my life—up to nine years of age in the worst neighborhood of all—in the worst possible area. That was my golden period. On the streets . . . boys who later went to the penitentiary, you know, committed all kinds of crimes. They were my great friends and my heroes and to this day I admire them.

I lived, d'you see, in Brooklyn. I had a cousin who lived in Manhattan, in the tenement district where I was born, on 85th Street in Yorkville. I'm, say, eight to twelve years old and when I come to visit my cousin, he says to his friends, one by one, "This is Henry, Henry Miller from Brooklyn." And they almost bow to me, the boys. I'm already made the leader of the gang, because I'm from another

HM treading water
in the pool

Dissolve from "Insomnia"
series watercolors
to a woman's face to
a photo of HM's mother

Henry was 76 years old when we started to work on this scene. His energy was overwhelming, and quite wore out the crew, despite the arthritis

His grandfather came to the States from Bavaria in Germany. He left the old country to avoid military service.

662 Driggs Avenue,
B'klyn,
where I spent the first
nine Years of my
life — my first
Paradise on earth!

Bet - Photos

1063 Decatur St. B'klyn - bet. Bushwick + Evergreen Aves. 1900-19
P.S. 85 - Evergreen Ave. & Covert St. - 1900 - 1905
Tromme's Beer Garden - opposite Entrance to Evergreen Cemetery
  (Bushwick Ave.) - 1900 - 1910
181 Devoe St. (nr. Graham Ave.) - Home of Cora Seward - 1905 - 1913
The Unique (Burlesk House - "The Barn") - Grand St. nr. Driggs Ave. 1890 - 19
The Police Station - Bedford Ave Cor. North 1st - 1890 - 1900
Presbyterian Church - Driggs Ave + South 3rd St. - 1890 - 1900
Driggs Ave. - from Grand St. to North 2nd St. (Metropolitan Ave) - 1890 - 19
Metropolitan Ave. (North 2nd St.) from Driggs Ave to River and a few block
  the other way - 1890 - 1900
P.S. 7 (?) - Driggs Ave. + North 5th St. - 1890 - 1900
The Tin Factory - North 1st St. bet. Bedford + Driggs Aves - 1890 - 1900
The Gayety Burlesk — Lorimer St. & B'way - 1910 - 1915
The Follies Theatre - Graham Ave. & 2nd Ave. New York 1913 - 1920
Minsky's Burlesk - Houston St. & 2nd Ave. - 1890 - 1900
Fillmore Place - Bet. Driggs Ave. + Roebling St. - 1890 - 1900
The Kindergarten - Corner Fillmore Pl. + Roebling St - 1890 - 1900
Corse Payton's Theatre - Marcy Ave. - 1905 - 1915
The Fountain - Bedford Ave near Broadway - 1890 - 1900
The Amphion Theatre — right at the Fountain — " "
91 Remsen St. (Borough Hall) - 1920 - 25
Montague St. Library - Borough Hall - 1905 - 1915
Clinton Avenue - nr. Myrtle Ave. - 1 block of the swell neighborhood
  1925 - 1930
Clinton Street - nr. Myrtle Ave (?) - 1925 - 1930
Henry St. nr. Love Lane - 1st house (brown stone stoop next to grocer,
  corner Love Lane) 1927-30
Sackett St. - going toward water - 1905 - 1915
Willow Place (B'klyn Heights) - 1900 - 1910
Grand Street - from Driggs Ave. to the Ferry - 1890 - 1900
Ferry Slip & Saloons - foot of Broadway - 1890 - 1900
Ulmer Park - 1890 - 1900
(?) Bensonhurst + 1900 - 1925
Glendale, L.I. - Laubscher's Saloon - 1898 - 1912
The Star Burlesk - Fulton St. nr. Borough Hall - 1915 - 1920
The Empire Burlesk - Broadway nr. DeKalb Ave (?) - 1912 - 1920
Roseland Dance Hall - B'way + (?) St. New York - 1912 - 1920
(?) The Greek Dance Hall (name) - almost opposite The Roseland 1922 - 1925
Eastern District High School - Marcy Ave. - 1905 - 1912
Primary School - North 1st St. bet. Driggs Ave. + Bedford 1914 - 19
Sargents' School of Arms - Columbus Circle, New York 1912 - 1918
The Tailor Shop - 5 West 31st St. New York 1916 - 1925
The Cycle Path - to Coney Island - Prospect Park - 1905 - 1910
The Turn Verein - Bushwick Ave. + Gates Ave. - 1900 - 1918
  (Driving Square) Weirfield St. + Knickerbocker Ave. (?)
Presbyterian Church Cor. St. 1909 - 1913
The Broadway Theatre - B'way + Graham Ave 1898 - 1902
The Novelty Theatre - Driggs Ave. + South 5th St. - 1925 - 1927
The Speak Easy - Perry St. nr. Hudson - 1927 - 28
The Roman Tavern (Greenwich Village) - MacDougal + 3rd St. (?) New York 1919 - 1925
Café Royal - 2nd Ave. + 12th (?) St. - New York - 1925 - 1928
The Pepper Pot (Greenwich Village) - Restaurant 1912 - 1920
Hamilton St. Ferry 1920 - 1925
Flatiron Bldg. - 23rd St + B'way, New York - 1904 - 1910
Herald Square Theatre - 35th St. + B'way, New York - 1904 - 1910
New York Herald (newspaper) Bldg. 35th + B'way. " " 1910 - 1925
The Brooklyn Bridge 1905 - 1910
Wallabout Market, Brooklyn 1900 - 1910
Geo. C. Tilyou's Steeplechase, Coney Island — 1900 - 1910

A typical Brooklyn
Street leading to
the waterfront.

House of my first
love — Cora Seward —
181 Devoe St.
Brooklyn, N.Y.

Triangle where the
Fountain used to be.
Where Sunday morn-
ings the cyclists
gathered to begin
their spin to Pros-
pect Park and
Coney Island.

neighborhood. They bring me things that they steal. We have rock fights together in the lot with rocks.

I tell a story where I killed one boy. I never went to the police, naturally. I came home, and I got rye bread from his mother, huh! . . . It was a wonderful tender neighborhood. Tender with violence. Again, American. You know, such warmth, and then this ferocity for no reason—I can't understand. . . .

My sister was a moron, she was born half-witted. She had the intelligence of a child of eight or ten. And she was a great burden in my life because I had to defend her when the kids called "Crazy Loretta, crazy Loretta," making fun of her, pulling her hair, Oh terrible. And I'm always chasing these kids and fighting with them, y'know. There was never any conversation with my sister—she drove me crazy. She can talk, but she talks a mile a minute about trivia. It makes sense, but it's about little things and it has no continuity, no point. A little thing here, a leaf, a tree (*laugh*) do y'see what I mean? After an hour with her I was nearly nuts, batty y'know, with this conversation.

And she had the faculty of crying easily over nothing, maybe out of joy, but silent tears, she didn't cry loudly, they just flew down silent, they just poured down her face and you never knew why. You'd ask her why, and she might say, "I'm happy." It was all very emotional. No continuous thing either; but she has a memory, greater than mine or anyone I know. Memory! She has songs, the titles of music, operas; she can remember back any time, any place, this girl, anything she's heard or read she can tell you about it.

I came to get my sister years later when my mother was dying, and she was a skeleton—my mother treated her like a slavy—she was walking around with pails and brushes mopping the floor and washing the walls. My mother used to think this was good for her. This kid couldn't go to school because she just couldn't learn, so they sent her home and my mother started to teach her. My mother was terrible. She used to crack her on the head; she'd say, "How much is two times two?" My sister would be frantic and say "Five, no, seven—no, three." And bang-bang; my mother would turn to me and say, "Why did I have to bear this cross? What did I do to be punished?" Asking me, a little boy, "Why did God punish me?" You can see what kind of mother this was. Huh. Stupid . . . terrible . . . terrible.

Now I never told you much about my father. My relations with him were rather cool while I worked in the tailor shop because my mother hoped I could prevent him from drinking, see. Keep tabs on him and all that. It was only later he was always wonderful. . . . And he believed in what I was doing, though he never read anything, dontcha'know. He said, go to it, go ahead, and all right, hope you make out.

Then, of course, he became ill. He gave up drink suddenly—all of a sudden, like that. And that was his downfall. When he did that he became ill. Up to then he had been in good health.

Loretta died not long ago, in a rest home in Monterey. Henry used to visit her every week or so when he lived in Big Sur.

(opposite page)
Henry, extreme left, with his sister Loretta, his mother, and his father. Henry is 8 or 9.

me in bottom, center, row,
in graduation day photo.
I was 13 years old. The
elementary school was P.S. 85
on Covert St. + Evergreen Ave.,
Brooklyn. Since demolished.

Photo of 1063 Decatur St. B'klyn,
where I lived from 10 to 21 years
of age. I am about 15 or 16
in this picture. In my books
I refer to this street as "The
Street of Early Sorrows."
The house was torn down some
years ago to make way for a
recreation center in what's
now a black ghetto.

And he was a man who had great friends. Everyone spoke highly of him—what a wonderful man he was, you know—in the tailor shop.

My father was drunk every day, you see. He went over toward noontime to have his first drink (*laughs*) at that wonderful Hotel Wolcott. He wanted me to grow up and take over the business, and so he would say, "You come over for lunch." I'd have gorgeous lunches there but I never drank a thing. I never took it. I was against it all. I would stand at the bar there with him and all his cronies. They're laughing and joking and "Henry," they ask me, "what are you drinking today?" And I'd say, "Water," y'know, huh. And they'd all laugh. Then I'd get angry and I'd glare at them. I remember once having a fight with a Frenchman there who insulted my father. Because my father was drunk and he was calling him all kinds of names. And I went up to him and I grabbed him, see, and they're all drinking y'know. And I considered them all a bunch of bums, and I'm in fine physical shape. Geez, I just grabbed him by the neck, I knocked him against the bar, I got him down on the floor, and I began choking him to death. They had to pull my hands—tear my hands—off him, I was killing him—I was really killing him—yeah (*laugh*).

I wan'na tell you about that: I have violence, great violence, in me, yeah. I'm afraid to get angry. That's why I'm so nice and peaceful. When I lose my head I go completely haywire, you know. I could do anything.

As a boy my father never finished school, sitting on the bench making clothes with his father. I never did that. When I went to his shop, I'm supposed to learn how to cut clothes, patterns, and all that. But I never did; instead of that I used to stand and talk for hours while my father's drinking at the bar. And no customers 'cause customers came in rarely, y'know; you only needed one or two suits a day. Sometimes days went by. These men ordered eight, nine suits at a time. Big money y'know.

The cutter was a Jewish immigrant from Poland whom I liked very very much—I mention him in the books. We'd stand there and talk while he'd cut and trace the pattern; he's supposed to be teaching me tailoring, but I never learned. And he was interested in literature. He knew Russian and Yiddish literature very well. Told me all about the ghettoes of Europe, y'know, that life—the folklore, the cabala—we went into all these things. Talked for hours every day, y know, with this man. It was great.

And sometimes I'd go into what you call the busheling room. That's the room where they pressed the clothes, and they sat on a bench too

Henry's father was a gentleman's tailor. He made carefully and beautifully sewn suits for the rich. His shop was off Fifth Avenue, in the 30's, in Manhattan.

to bushel is to finish, alter or repair garments - especially men's suits - according to Webster III.

and sewed, coats, y'know. There were three Jews, they were very interesting to me. One was an opera singer. Real enough. I would open the windows there, so that in those loft buildings there they could hear him, and I'd say, "Now Reuben, start in, from *Pagliacci* or a Russian opera like *Boris Godunov*, y'know, or anything. He had a voice . . . tremendous . . . a tenor, like a Caruso, you know, and soon (*he claps softly*) we'd hear them clapping from all the windows there. . . . "More, more," do y'know. And if my father happened to walk in then drunk, or a customer walked in, they wondered what the hell is this, y'see (*laughs*).

Naturally the business went to hell. And the wonderful thing was that when it went to hell, my father's stone broke, these little Jewish tailors offered to help him with his debts—pawn their things, give watches, er, all their savings, and everything. And I told them, "Don't do it, because it's a waste. It's gone. We can't do anything you know." But that's how wonderful they were, yeah. . . . It was a great experience there.

And I met a number of famous people there, one who encouraged me very much. One day, who walks in, to my great surprise? Frank Harris. Frank Harris was living in Washington Square, and he wanted some clothes. (*Laughs.*) My father, of course, never heard of him, but I had read Frank Harris already and I was tickled to death, y'see, to meet him. And my father, . . . well, my father had no use for artists. He thought they were all crackbrained with no money and all that. Frank Harris wanted a suit to go on a yacht. A light, gay material—and my father shows him material with broad stripes like a minstrel-show man would wear. Frank Harris began to laugh, and my father says, "You're a writer, you know, you're a bohemian." Imagine!

Well, Frank Harris was great. He soon discovered these little tailors in the back. He noticed that the cutter who fitted him was a very wonderful man. Got to talking, y'know, about Jewish literature, then about Shakespeare, then about the Bible, and then about Oscar Wilde. And he ordered these guys, "Come out, I want to talk to you." Talked to them just like equals. It was so marvelous. . . . They said to me afterwards, I'll never forget it, "Who is that great man?" they said, "Who is that wonderful great man?" (*Laughs.*)

I used to be the errand boy as well as the assistant to my father next in line. When night came, I delivered clothes on my arm, wrapped in paper, to wealthy homes—by the back door. And I had to deliver a suit to Frank Harris. Beautiful apartment, Washington Square, y'know, one of those old buildings. He says, "Come in." I walk in.

Henry, seated center, is 18 or 19. at his right is his sister Loretta.

Henry at 21 or 22 years.

Frank Harris, who wanted a suit to wear on a yacht.

He's in bed with a woman! (*Laughs.*) He gets up. He has only his pajama top on. He never wore underwear, by the way, a thing my father couldn't stand. "Why should I wear underwear?" he'd say. And he asked me to help him on with his trousers. Can you imagine that scene? And me thinking: Now what can I ask him about writing?

Writing! . . .

Writing, y'know. . . .

(*Laugh.*) Well, did you ever get a chance to talk to him about writing?

Yes, I did. Oh, and later he published one of my things in a magazine he took over, a famous old magazine—I can't recall the name. And when I went to France, that time I left New York to go to Spain as I thought, my father had Frank Harris's address in the south; And I wrote to Frank Harris and told him I was coming to Paris and I'm writing and so on, and I got a letter back; he said, "Why don't you come down here to Nice? I have a big house. You can live here free." I never did it, but that was how wonderful he was.

Well, I hated the business, I had no interest in it at all, don't y'know. I couldn't see myself becoming a tailor. All I got out of that two, three, or four years was a knowledge, a feel, of woolens and silks—good material—and fancy vest buttons. Jesus, y'know, they wore fancy vest buttons in those days. But I know a good piece of material when I touch it. And I know when a suit fits properly and all that.

Snyder
HvM:

From a letter to Lawrence Durrell

". . . I wanted nothing more of God than the power to write. Yes, this began in my late teens, I imagine. In my early twenties, confined to my father's shop, a slave to the most idiotic kind of routine imaginable, I broke out—inside. Inwardly, I was a perpetual volcano. I will never forget the walks to and from my father's shop every day: the tremendous dialogues I had with my characters, the scenes I portrayed, and so on. And never a line of any of this ever put to paper. Where would you begin if you were a smothered volcano?"

All this time, in the back of my head, I'm the writer who is never writing. I made one attempt to write with a little broken pencil once, can you imagine? No, I wrote a page and gave it up. I said I would never be able to write. Well, but nevertheless, it was there, it was in me. Dialogues with characters, I can remember; I can say I wrote several books in this period I worked for my father, because I did the same thing at night. I'd walk back down to that station, do y'know. This meant I'd walk through the Bowery, too, part of the way, and Union Square and Madison Square Garden, which was a beautiful building then, do you remember? And then, on that walk also, I

stopped at a certain shop, a framing shop, where I got interested in painting. Because there I saw my first Japanese prints. I used to stand there, and I saw reproductions of Chagall and Utrillo and Matisse and all that. That was really the first beginnings of my interest in painting, do y'know.

Listen, you have no idea when I first began to paint—how it was that I began. I had a boyhood friend who was my friend up until a few years ago when he died. I knew him from the age of 10. Now the difference between us was that at 10 he already was a talented artist, and he stood out in our school. At certain periods, the teacher would say—go to the blackboard, Emil, and draw us this or that. Now this poor fellow became, at a very early age, a commercial artist because he had to support a mother, a father, a sister, and whatnot. And this was his death and ruination as an artist. He never became a good artist; but he was a lover of art. We spent whole nights—like he would come at 8:00 o'clock and it would last until 2:00 o'clock and 3:00 o'clock in the morning—he would bring art books . . . the Old Masters from all periods . . . and we would talk about them, reverently look at and discuss their work.

This was a very important period in my life, you know. I had not yet done a thing. I didn't think I could, you know. I was always thrown out of the class for being incompetent. Don't come into the art class because you can't even draw a straight line! And I knew this and I was always afraid to take a pencil or brush. It was through seeing George Grosz's album—the cover had a picture of a man on it, which is still in that new edition. . . . One night, I don't know what ever possessed me, I copied that and I copied it very well. And I said, by God, maybe I can draw and paint—and I began, like that. But let's not forget, my friend Emil provided the wonderful background for me—the feeling for art, the reverence and all that. I'll never forget it. . . . Emil Schnellock of Brooklyn. He was a painter. But, as an artist, a failure. You know where he ended up? Teaching art in a girls' college in Virginia—Professor of Art. And he was a good one for that, but he never became a good artist. The thing is that I think his commercial art work killed him.

He would say to me when I first began painting—Henry, if only I could be loose and reckless like that! And he'd try and he'd show me . . . and it wasn't at all that way. He knew too much to be reckless, do you see?

Now all this time I think I'll never be a writer. But I was reading all the current authors of the day. For instance, I remember that John Dos Passos was quite a name then already. But he was not much older than

Dissolve to series of HM watercolors

Henry: "George Grosz's pictures were brutal; they were meant to be that. A condemnation of the German nation, the people, the whole people, were condemned forever. I don't think even Goya could have done for the Spaniards what Grosz did against the Germans. He left an indelible mark on them. they are condemned forever, for all eternity, in Grosz's paintings; that's how I feel.

the Xerxes Society

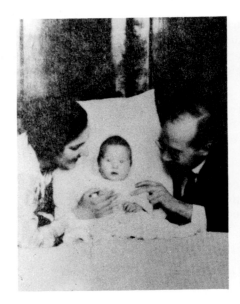

Emil Schnellock   *Knut Hamsun*

me, or maybe the same age. And, already, he had made it. He had been in the war and he had written a book about the war, do you recall? And I used to read these men, and I'd say to myself, "Jesus, I think I could do as well as that," y'know. But never do it.

The Xerxes Society . . . the group of friends. It was a social and an athletic club. We staged running matches, boxing matches. We were very much interested in fight games. When Sweet Caporal were all the vogue, they gave out cards, of soubrettes of the burlesque, and of fighters; and among them, my heroes Corbett and John L. Sullivan, Terry McGovern, Jack Johnson. I was crazy about the bicycle, and crazy enough to pace the six-day riders . . . from Prospect Park, along a beautiful gravel path, six miles right down to Coney Island, to the water; and, since I was a kid, and I had the heart and could spare the strength, they used me. It was nice to see them all there. They gathered at a little fountain, talked, fixed their wheels, greased the chains, fixed the handlebars. And then we set out, leisurely, get faster and faster, you see; this was their workout.

While still working for my father I married, my first marriage; had a child. And then, at night, I would come home—I had that big rolltop desk that you're curious about, this rolltop desk, y'know, which is a pigeonhole desk. (*Reading.*) "This is the desk that had been in the old man's tailoring establishment for the last fifty years, which had given birth to many bills and many groans, which had housed strange souvenirs in its compartments, and which, finally, I had filched from him when he was ill and away from the tailoring establishment. "And now it stood in the middle of the floor in our huge lugubrious parlor in the third floor of a respectable brownstone house in the dead center of the most respectable neighborhood in Brooklyn. And I put all the extra chairs we had around it in a circle and then I sat down comfortably and I put my feet on the desk and dreamed of what I could write if I could write. All the pigeonholes were empty and all the drawers were empty. There wasn't a thing on the desk or in it except a sheet of white paper on which I found it impossible to put so much as a pothook."—I would sit there then and write at night. It was nothing very good. I never even tried to sell any of that stuff, you know.

"And then there was that curious business about Knut Hamsun. The one writer I started out to write like, to be like. How much time and thought I have given to that man's work—in the past. How I struggled to phrase my thoughts as he did. And without the least success. . . ."

After this period with my father, somehow or other, I don't know how I got out of it all. Maybe he had to give up business, I forget exactly, now, at this minute. Anyhow then I had a number of jobs in between. Like I was assistant editor to a mail-order house, like the Charles Williams, I was the editor of that big catalogue they put out. And I was fired one

Photo of Xerxes Society

Dissolve to wall with photos of prizefighters

Dissolve to HM bicycling

1918, the first of five marriages, to Beatrice Sylvas Wickens. Their daughter, Barbara, lives in Pasadena. We were present, cameras and all, at the fifth marriage, to Hoki.

"To be a writer was like saying I was going to be a saint or a martyr or God. It was just as remote as that."

day because I got caught typing out from Nietzsche's *Antichrist,* you know,¹ while working on company time.

And I was caught red-handed—fired. I went over to say goodbye to the man who gave me the job, and he says "What happened?" and I tell him. He shakes his head. "Listen," he says, "wait a minute." He called his secretary and dictated some letters to friends praising the shit out of me, to get another job. Then he reaches into his pocket and says, "I don't know what they're giving you here, but let me give you this." It was a fifty-dollar bill and wishing me luck and all that. I was crying when I left, and went outside weeping.

Well, I had a number of jobs like that. I was in a bank, the Federal Reserve Bank; what am I doing there? Working a machine to check errors in the machine do you know, figures. I didn't know anything about . . . And I was fired from that because they discovered three months after I'm working that I had once been living with this older woman, the widow whom I lived with for three years. And they er, thought there was a possibility she might beg me for money and I might steal money from them. I never saw money in this job. (*Laughs.*)

Dissolve to HM in bathrobe sitting under tree at the side of the pool

Robert Snyder:
HM:

I was married then and already had a child. I tried to get a job as a messenger boy, y'know, at Western Union and they turned me down. I was so angry I couldn't sleep all night, and I worked out a plan to see the president of Western Union.

Did you get to see the president?

No, the vice-president, and I say, "Why, why can't I get the lowest job, on earth—a messenger boy?" They finally sent me over to the manager who listens to me for an hour or more and instead of giving me a job as messenger he says, "Mr. Miller, why don't you take over the personnel department and be the manager of the messenger department? First, in order to give you experience, work as a messenger for a while. You'll get paid as the employment manager—nobody will know it but us two—but you'll work as a messenger."

So I went from office to office and got the lay of the land. And then I knew only too well what that life was. To tell you the truth, I could hardly stand it. It was winter—snow and ice on the ground. I came home the first night as though my feet were made of broken bones and glass. I went to bed groaning from the pain.

Well, I discovered New York. I had been living in it all my life, and then came my great discovery of New York when I was with Western. Four and a half years employment manager. And after I finished my day's work, I would eat dinner with the detective of the company. He'd come at that hour, and we'd go out together and visit the

telegraph offices—we'd be looking for crooks and runaway boys and all that. That brought us into every nook and cranny there in New York. Every dive, all the Bowery, the East Side, up to Harlem. Everything. I knew it all like a book, y'know.

I was due at work every morning at eight o'clock. I seldom arrived at eight (*laughs*), but when I did, there'd be a whole mob waiting for me in the anteroom you know, waiting to be hired. Because we had largely the scum, the riff-raff, don't y'know. And among them were great kids. Lots of them were crooks. I didn't mind it too much. But they were all liars. Nearly all young kids are liars, you know, it's amazing. They—and the best, the model ones who look so beautiful and pious, y'know, and good—they were the worst ones always. See, I visited their homes often at night. To find out what was what. Kids would come you know, begging for the job and then saying, well, we have nothing to eat at home, my father is ill and this and this and that. I'd go there. Then I'd try to get the charitable organizations interested. And that took so long. I was paying out of my own money (that) I'd give them, I'd keep them going, you see. Then I borrowed from my associates in the office. I was always in debt, the whole time at that job. I owed everybody, helping out these kids.

But I was married a few years I guess, when finally I ran into "Mona," in my books, you know, in the dance hall, and we were caught in bed one morning when I thought my wife had gone on a vacation. (*Laugh.*) She'd done that to trap me and there she found me in bed you see, in my own house, with witnesses and everything. So I left her immediately and went to live with June—"Mona." And it was through my new wife that I got the courage to make my final decisions and to live by them.

June still worked at the dance hall, and she used to say to me, "Look, give up that job; Start to write," y'know. She pushed me into it. And one day I did quit. I quit just like that. Just came into the office one morning—there were forty or fifty applicants for messenger jobs— and I said to my assistant, "You tell the boss I'm quitting and I don't want my salary"—there was two weeks coming—"and I don't want anything. I want to get out." And I walked out. I had a little briefcase with me, I'll never forget it. I walked up Broadway, it was about ten in the morning, feeling like the happiest man that I'm no longer gonna work for anybody. That was my idea. Now I'm gonna write, do y'see. But that was a beautiful walk. Looking at all those poor bastards who are working, struggling, selling and buying things, y'know.

That is a marvel. I can't get over it, how marvelous it is to feel detached from this mechanism, this cogwheel that we're all in, don't y'know; and you say, "there it is spinning and I'm not of it, I don't

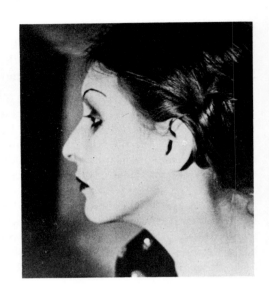

Mona - June

belong." And you look on them like insects y'know, huh? That's right. That's all they are, really and true; they are working insects, these creatures. It doesn't matter if they become presidents or vice-presidents of banks or whatnot. They're still in that category—but they're master insects, that's all. (*Laughter.*)

But then began my ten years of misery, y'know, trying to sell my work.

"Since I wasn't really meant to be a writer, not a born writer like Larry Durrell, all that was permitted me was to give expression to this business of writing and being a writer; in short, my own private struggles with the problem. . . . Out of the lack I made my song."

Letter to Alfred Perlès.

This desire to write must have been strong in me from way back y'know. But I had no confidence in my ability to write. That was the thing—I had absolutely no confidence. A very strange thing. So I began by writing . . . oh, I thought I would start like exercises, and I'd write about things I was interested in, people, events—I'd go to meet people. I went to the editor of Funk and Wagnall's dictionary, and wrote an article, a long beautiful one about words which I sold to *Liberty* magazine, that five-cent magazine. They liked me there, they almost gave me a job as assistant editor, and they paid me, that was fabulous—I think I got three hundred dollars, which was a big sum in those days. But they never printed it. And I would ask every now and then. "It's too good," they'd say. Too good, how do you like that? Finally I caught on to the idea, y'know, there were magazines like *Snappy* stories, like our *Playboy* thing, in a way, today. I wrote one or two, had no luck and I got the idea to send in my wife, who was beautiful, with these things, and, of course, they sold. After I sold two or three I thought, why should I write new things? I'd go to their back files, ten years, twelve years ago, pull out their own story and change the beginning and end and the names of the characters, and I'd sell it to them. This is what they loved. It was their own stuff (*laughs.*)

At that time we moved. I told you about Henry Street, Hick Street, Clinton Street—I lived in so many parts of Brooklyn. But 91 Remsen was where we really started off, when I really settled down. Now I'm writing and so on. That was a beautiful place, y'know, aristocratic. We lived in Japanese style, long mattresses on the floor, beautiful little art objects. We were living as though we had money, and we didn't pay the rent for about four months. And the owner of the place and his wife were Virginians, and one day he just knocked at the door. I was alone, supposedly writing.

He said, "Mr. Miller, could I talk to you?" We sat down on the bed; he said "Sit down here." Then he said, "Mr. Miller, you know, my wife and I, we like you and your wife, but I think," he said, "you're a bit of

a dreamer. (*Laughs.*) You know we can't go on forever keeping you, y'see. And we'd like to have you. We don't ask you to pay the back rent—we know you don't have any money—but could you please, uh, vacate in a reasonable time?"

He was so lovely, this man, y'know. I felt so bad, and I promised him all, all. I said, "I'm certainly going to pay you back, do y'know, you've been so kind." 'Course I never did. (*Laughs.*) But I remember that one time my conscience was touched, don't y'know.

Yes, now and then—my wife wasn't working maybe and, of course, I wasn't selling anything—we'd have to separate, and I'd go home to live with my parents and she with her parents. That was frightful. When I'd go home to live with my parents my mother would say, "If anybody comes, a neighbor or one of our friends, y'know, hide that typewriter and you go in the closet, don't let them know you're here." I used to stay in that closet sometimes over an hour, the camphor-ball smell choking me to death, hidden among the clothes, hidden y'know, so that she wouldn't have to tell her neighbors or relatives that her son is a writer. All her life she hated this, that I'm a writer. She wanted me to be a tailor and take over the tailorshop, y'know. It was a frightful thing—this is like a crime I'm committing, I'm a criminal, y'know. This standing in the closet, . . . I'll never forget the smell of camphor, do y'know. We used it plentifully. (*Laughs.*)

I guess it was a year or two later that we had occasion to go into the studios of KCET, Channel 28 in Los Angeles, to do what might be a pilot for a mini series, "Henry Miller Reads and Muses." Henry kept complaining that some dignified actor should be reading from his work—someone like, say, Gregory Peck. We set him up at a rolltop desk, put a brass spitoon beside it, surrounded it with turn-of-the-century stuffed chairs. In preparation for one of these sessions, I asked him which book was his favorite, to which he replied after a moment's hesitation: The Colossus of Maroussi. *And which his favorite story or character? Without an instant's pause:* Tante Mele. *So he read that long, typically tragi-comic section on Tante Mele from "The Tailor Shop" in* Black Spring.

When I was editing The Henry Miller Odyssey *much later, and it began to be apparent that just two major revisitings, to Paris and Brooklyn, would already make a long film, I thought it would tie things together nicely to end Part I with this reading because of its vivid description of that part of his life as well as the expression of his devotion to the innocence of angels, saints, and the insane.*

We screened the final rough cut for him while he continued to grumble throughout that a proper actor, a reader, should have been reading his literature, and he wanted it deleted. I reminded him of his frequent

Henry was getting chilly now, so we broke for a snack. Meticulously, he put on the kettle with just the right amount of water, took the necessaries from the refrigerator, from the silverware drawer, and carefully laid it all out on place mats on the dining table. I was introduced to an oft-repeated ritual.

To my astonishment, he capped it off by putting down, on the right side of his setting, a serviette, a real linen napkin, rolled up in a wooden napkin ring, with "H.M." burned into it. And, after the snack, folding the napkin precisely in half, and rolling it up and into the holder, the process was just as carefully reversed.

disclaimers of his work as "Literature," and I steadfastly insisted—as I had before and have since—that no actor—not Humphrey Bogart, not even Jimmie Gleason, let alone Gregory Peck—could do it justice. Only Henry Miller could read Henry Miller.

However, always merry and bright. If it was before the war, and the thermometer down to zero or below, if it happened to be Thanksgiving Day, New Year's, or a birthday, or just any old excuse to get together, then off we'd trot the whole family to join the other freaks who made up the family tree. It always seemed astounding to me how jolly they were in our family in spite of all the calamities that were always threatening. Jolly in spite of everything. There was cancer, dropsy, incest, paralysis, tapeworm, abortions, triplets, idiots, drunkards, ne'er-do-wells, fanatics, sailors, tailors, watchmakers, scarlet fever, whooping cough, meningitis, running ears, chorea, stutterers, jailbirds, dreamers, storytellers, bartenders, and finally there was Uncle George and Tante Mele . The morgue, and the insane asylum. A merry crew and the table loaded with good things. . . .

No one knew that Tante Mele was going completely off her nut, that when we reached the corner she could leap forward like a reindeer and bite a piece out of the moon. At the corner she leaped forward like a reindeer and she shrieked. "The moon, the moon!" she cried, and with that her soul broke loose, jumped clean out of her body. . . . Out, out, to the moon, and nobody could think quick enough to stop it. Just like that it happened. In the twinkle of a star.

And now I'm going to tell you what those bastards said to me. . . .

They said, *"Henry, you take her to the asylum tomorrow, and don't tell them that we can afford to pay for her."*

Fine! Always merry and bright! The next morning we boarded the trolley together and we rode out into the country. If Mele asked where we were going, I was to say "To visit Aunt Monica." But Mele didn't ask any questions. She sat quietly beside me and pointed to the cows now and then. She saw blue cows and green ones. She knew their names. She asked what happened to the moon in the daytime. And did I have a piece of liverwurst by any chance?

During the journey I wept—I couldn't help it When people are too good for this world they have to be put under lock and key. There's something wrong with people who are too good. It's true Mele was lazy. She was born lazy. It's true that Mele was a poor housekeeper. It's true Mele didn't know how to hold on to a husband when they got her one. When Paul ran off with a woman from Hamburg, Mele sat in

Dissolve to HM
at rolltop desk, reading
from Black Spring

Henry reading the Tante Melia
episode from _Black Spring_
- at his "rolltop desk".

a corner and wept. The others wanted her to do something—put a bullet in him, raise a rumpus, sue for alimony. Mele sat quiet. Mele wept. Mele hung her head. She was like a pair of torn socks that are kicked around here, there, everywhere. Always turning up at the wrong moment. . . .

And now she's very tranquil and she calls the cows by their first name. The moon fascinates her. She has no fear because I'm with her and she always trusted me. I was her favorite. Even though she was a half-wit she was good to me. The others were more intelligent, but their hearts were bad.

Sometimes when she was fired from a job, they used to send me to fetch her. Mele never knew her way home. And I remember how happy she was every time she saw me coming. She would say innocently that she wanted to stay with us. Why couldn't she stay with us? I used to ask myself that over and over. Why couldn't they make a place for her by the fire, let her sit there and dream if that's what she wanted to do? Why must everybody *work*—even the saints and the angels? Why must half-wits set a good example?

I'm thinking now that after all it may be good for Mele where I'm taking her. No more work. Just the same, I'd rather that they had made a corner for her somewhere.

Walking down the gravel path towards the big gates, Mele becomes uneasy. Even a puppy knows when it's being carried to a pond to be drowned. Mele is trembling now. At the gate they are waiting for us. The gate yawns. Mele is on the inside, I am on the outside. They are trying to coax her along. They are gentle with her now. They speak to her so gently. But Mele is terror stricken. She turns and runs toward the gate. I am still standing there. She puts her arms through the bars and clutches at my neck. I kiss her gently on the forehead. Gently I unlock her arms. The others are going to take her again. I can't bear seeing that. I must go. I must run. For a full minute however, I stand and look at her. Her eyes seem to have grown enormous. Two great round eyes, full and black as the night, staring at me uncomprehendingly. No maniac can look that way. No idiot can look that way. Only an angel or a saint. . . .

When I ran away from the gate I stopped beside a high wall, and burying my head in my arms, my arms against the wall, I sobbed as I had never sobbed since I was a child. Meanwhile they were giving Mele a bath and putting her into regulation dress; they parted her hair in the middle, brushed it down flat and tied it into a knot at the nape of the neck. Thus no one looks exceptional. All have the same crazy look, whether they are half crazy, or three-quarters crazy, or just slightly cracked. When you say, "May I have pen and ink to write a

letter?" they say "yes" and they hand you a broom to sweep the floor. If you pee on the floor absent-mindedly you have to wipe it up. You can sob all you like, but you mustn't violate the rules of the house. A bughouse has to run in orderly fashion just as any other house. . . .

When Mele stood at the gate with her eyes so bright and round her mind must have traveled back like an express train. Everything must have leaped to her mind at once. Her eyes were so big and bright as if they saw more than they could comprehend. Bright with terror, and beneath the terror a limitless confusion. That's what made them so beautifully bright. You have to be crazy to see things so lucidly, so all at once. If you're great you can stay that way, and people will believe in you, swear by you, turn the world upside-down for you. But if you're only partly great or just a nobody, then what happens to you is lost.

Letter to Alfred Perlès

"What I needed most desperately was a voice with which to express my grief and abondonment. That is how I came to write. My thought was simple and direct. My prayer, I should say, for it virtually took that form. 'Give me, O God,' is what I kept saying, 'the power to express this anguish which afflicts me. Let me tell it to the world, for I can't bear to keep it locked up in my own breast.''

The Paris Years

I was now a regular at chez Miller Saturday and/or Sunday Ping-Pong bashes, and dropping in occasionally for a swim, a chat, a drink or two, a turn on the "vélo." I became aware during this period that he was in love and courting (and I mean courting, in the Victorian sense). Joe Gray, privy to the clandestine activities of this very active old man, confirmed my suspicions: She was a young Japanese pianist-singer-entertainer, and it was getting serious. And after days of backing and filling, discussions, tergiversations (a fifty-dollar word, HM would interject) plans un-planned and arabesqued pros and cons, he blurted out: "Hoki and I are going to be married—that'll be my fifth marriage; it's crazy."

Concurrently, the Westwood Art Association, which had had a couple of shows of his watercolors, announced a members' charter flight to Europe—first stop, Paris, for an exhibition of Henry's watercolors there. And Henry and Hoki would go on the trip as their honeymoon (don't know which was the cause, which the effect) and Henry urged me to come along to film Paris Revisited. This was in earnest—spelled m-o-n-e-y. He'd lend me the money. That did it (and put a rope around my neck). As the newspapers had it:

Robert Snyder will be Miller's shadow during the Westwood Art Association's junket to Europe this Fall (for a Paris exhibit of his watercolors) filming a documentary on Miller.

Confusion broke in like a tidal wave: arrangements for the wedding (does he have all his divorce papers in order? what's the status of her citizenship?); for the reception; for the trip (he packs as carefully as he sets the table); for the filming. In the midst of informally filming a little session of Henry at the watercolor desk, he's writing "A Memo to Myself."

That memo I wrote to myself today. September 17th, 1918, after a bloody hectic few weeks such as I don't think I've been through in ages. Here it is from the top of my head:

(1)

Memo to
myself
9/17/18*

If we get thru this bloody business
we can thank all the gods there
are, plus the Supreme Being,
and Maha Kali, mother of all

what are we here for if not
to enjoy life eternal, solve what
problems we can, give light,
peace and joy to our fellow-
man, and leave this dear
fucked-up planet a little healthier
than when we were born. Who
knows what other planets we
will be visiting and what new
wonders there will unfold?
We certainly live more than once. Do we
ever _die_ — that is the question.

In any case, thank God we are
alive and of the stars — into all
eternity

Amen!

Henry Miller

It could have applied to any or all of the circumstances which were, Laocoon-like, encoiling him. "Getting through that bloody business" could have applied to the filming. I used it with that implication at the end of the Odyssey. But on reflection, I wondered whether it referred to the confusion surrounding the marriage: note the date. It was most unusual for such a precise man to write 1918 instead of 1968. He mentioned during the earliest period of filming "The Brooklyn Years" that his first marriage took place when the draft was announced in 1918. He ran into a friend who replied to his fears: "Get married, you silly bastard, and you'll be deferred." And he did.

Baylis and I did shadow and film him during his fifty-three-day most hectic trip to Europe—commencing with the vernissage of his Paris exhibition, then revisiting many of his old haunts in Paris as well as the homes and studios of friends and artists he knew back in the thirties, with a side trip to Provence. Larry Durrell had come up to Paris, of course, but invited us down to his place in Sommieres. And just places. The great list-maker provided me with a roster of his favorite places in Paris.

Forebodings of the madness that was to descend upon us were made evident on our arrival at Orly—Parisian and European press corps, photographers (European-style paparazzi), French TV crews and crews from Germany, Sweden, and Switzerland among others, mobbed us. After a small cordial reception, we fled to our respective hotels—in secrecy.

The following evening, the vernissage; the day having been spent moving to different rooms to muddy the trail. But the press has ways of buying tips from switchboard operators. When we looked out from the refuge of the hotel, we could see the hungry mob. We improvised a flying wedge around Henry and crossed over the avenue to the gallery—fighting off the press every inch of the way—and managed to get safely to the back office of the gallery via a side alley. This was a comfortable, if cramped, cubicle without a top.

The gallery was filled to capacity, crowds pushing to get in. Those on the inside climbed on chairs as well as each other, hanging over the wall of the cubicle to get a look at him. Henry was somewhat alarmed, and we were actually afraid that the thin walls would crash in on us. Daniel Gervis boldly went out and announced that unless the crowd thinned out a bit, M. Miller would not be able to join the reception. It never thinned, and after an hour's wait, getting hotter and hotter, we tried to sneak a message out to the lieutenant of the gendarmerie posted outside to provide us with safe-conduct back to the hotel.

After another half hour, we sent a more trusted messenger to get the first messenger, who, along with the lieutenant, had been tipped by the owner of the gallery to keep things humming and let the situation

Daniel Gervis 34 rue du Bac
vous prie d'honorer de votre
présence le vernissage de
l'exposition des gouaches d'

Henry Miller

vendredi 22 septembre à 17 h

22 septembre au 14 octobre

Arrival at Orly.

become a cause célèbre. Getting back across the avenue proved more terrifying than the first crossing—the whole crowd swarming around us when they discovered us halfway over. I felt a chill down my spine when I realized that the media would like him to—well, not drop dead, but maybe have a little stroke, or at least to fall, in order to capture the news.

In a day or so, we got back to normal, normal, that is, for a public hero (I hadn't realized his position in Europe): The newspaper kiosks were emblazoned with a magazine whose cover featured André Malraux, for the publication of his sensational Anti-Mémoires, and Miller, just for being there.

A watercolor and an etching by H.M.

Things settled down a bit: He did his things and we did our thing. By now we were part of the furniture, taken for granted. Baylis had begun to feel easier, more accepted by Henry. But, in Paris, if we were sitting in a bar with Brassai, say, every situation, exterior and interior, was new, unfamiliar ground. At home, back in California, we had gotten to know each room, each segment of the pool and garden, in our bones; we had even replaced some of the lighting fixtures' customary lamps—whether 75 watts or 250 watts—with 3200 K-temperature lamps suitable for color. Now, Baylis would move in, quite naturally, with his light meter.

"Verboten! Interdit!" Henry railed at me back at his hotel, when I took leave of him that night. "I thought we agreed—no light meters. . . ." I apologized for backsliding and slunk off.

When I got back to our hotel I gave Baylis hell: "Do you want to blow the whole deal?" He was most contrite, but reasserted his professional dignity: "Well, after all, you want a good image, don't you?" "No, Baylis, you want a 'good image'; we just want an 'image.' " (Oh, the Scylla-Charybdis of being producer-director or any hyphenated function.)

Happily, we got both an image and a good one. Later on, when the great Jean Renoir saw the film and sent me his beautiful letter of appreciation, he asked, "How were you able to get those shots? How did you find those places?" I answered, "We saw it over Henry's shoulders, with his eyes; and remember, M. Renoir, when you make a film, it is a big production, with 35mm equipment and a large crew. You couldn't squeeze into such places even if the civil authorities and the local citizenry permitted you to get there (nothing draws a crowd in swarms like the sight of a movie crew, with or without 'stars')." We were just two young tourists, and German and Japanese tourists normally carry more photographic gear than we did, going along with a couple of older tourists.

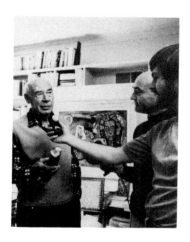

        Le film de Henry Miller c'est Paris. Si
j'ajoute à cette déclaration celle que Henry Miller
est aussi admirable à l'écran qu'il l'est dans la
vie vous comprendrez les raisons de mon intérêt.
Henry Miller fait partie de cette mince phalange qui
détient le pouvoir de discerner ce qui vaut la peine
d'être retenu et xxix cela sous les climats les
plus divers. Ce film est un hymne au génie personnel.
Il plaira à tous ceux qui n'ont pas abandonné une
certaine recherche de l'aristocratie.

                         Best regards,

                           Jean Renoir

For his autobiographical sketch
in *Americans Abroad* (1932),
Henry Miller wrote:
Born New York City, 1891.
No schooling. Was tailor,
personnel manager in a
large corporation,
ranchman in California,
newspaperman, hobo
and wanderer. Was a
6-day bike racer, a
concert pianist, and in
my spare time, I practice
sainthood. Came to Paris
to study vice.

Letter to Emil Schnellock,
a childhood friend from
grammar school days.

I told you already about Knut Hamsun and his effect on me. Incidentally, in the last part of *Nexus* I go into that . . . my love of Knut Hamsun—and Myrtle Avenue. I'm sitting on the bench there on Myrtle Avenue which is the goddamndest street of all streets in the world, remember?

Yeah.

And I think a quarter rolled down onto the ground and I begin this fantastic bit with a bum—in a Hamsunesque vein—telling him, "Pick it up," I said, "and listen, you know that isn't going to be enough, why don't you take a dollar?" He says, "All I wanted was a dime, that's all I'm asking you for." And I said, "But look, with a quarter you could get two drinks, y'know." . . . And he's beginning to edge away from me and I said, "Now, look, I'm going to leave a dollar here on the bench, and when I go away you can come back and pick it up." And he begins to think I'm a nut and begins to curse at me and swear, and he runs away from me. And I put the dollar on the bench here and tell him to come back and get it, y'know. And I'm telling him, y'know— here I'm sitting on the bench—how I could hand out lots of money now. I'm on my way to Europe on a big boat, y'see, and I'm going to live like a king. And the more I talk, the more he thinks I'm mad.

4 Anatole France Clichy, April 1932

Dear Emil,

No, I don't want to return to America, Nothing but a catastrophe could make me go back. This is my world and I knew it long, long ago, I only regret it took so long to make the decision. What a different person I would have been if at twenty-one I went to the Sorbonne, or at Alt Heidelberg, or to Seville or Madrid. Anywhere but City College. However it hasn't been too late. I will never become a European, but thank God I will never become an American. I'm one of those things you call an expatriate, a voluntary exile, I have no country, no frontiers, no taxes to pay, and no army to fight for. And I adore Franco. It's getting to the point where I will actually have to earn a living. I feel now as all the great vagabond artists must have felt: absolutely reckless, childish, irresponsible, unscrupulous, and overflowing with carnal vitality, vigor, ginger, etc. Always on the border of insanity due to worry, hunger etc. But shoving along day after day.

I got to Paris in 1930. I was there in 1928 first on a trip through all of Europe with no thought of remaining—just a holiday. I spent one year

going all over Europe, then we came back, remained in New York, and in 1930 I left my wife in New York and I landed in London with my wife's promise that she'd mail me money there . . . and I could get on to Paris. I had to borrow a ten-dollar bill at the last minute so I'd have something. . . .

Didn't you say, you go before—what did you say?—a driving wind, and get plumped down; but didn't you choose Paris or Europe?

Oh yes, I did. But in a way I hadn't chosen Paris; I intended to go to Spain. When I left New York it was with the intention of going to Spain—and I never got there, not until many years later.

No, I never had any thought of living in Paris. I had been there two years earlier and I wasn't so impressed with it, I must tell you. Isn't that strange? I think that I've never chosen a place in my life. I've only lived where, by accident, I've found myself, and force of circumstance kept me there and then I grew to like it, y'know, I adapted to it.

Fade in to HM looking
over Paris from the top
of Menilmontant

Jakob Gimpel was the only one of Henry's close California friends to be present. He participated in the California festivities, arrived in Paris the following day to commence a European tour, and played a bit of Henry's favourite, Scriabin, at the exhibit.

Flash forward: While we were celebrating his 80th birthday at UCLA, the Centre Culturel Americain at the American Embassy in Paris observed the occasion by presenting an exhibit, "Les Amis Parisiens de Henry Miller" (and running The Henry Miller Odyssey). *We filmed a little "singing telegram" by Henry.*

Dissolve to HM and
Braissaï walking into
Brassaï's studio. Int. studio
and apartment

"Brassai, the eye of Paris. It was in those early days that I used to go with him at night all over Paris, helping him carry his equipment and so on. And I got to see a great many parts of Paris I might never have seen through him. He knew Paris thoroughly. And what I remember then, the thing that everybody noticed, is his eyes. His eyes, really they protrude like the lens of a camera. You see, he had only begun to take up photography when I met him; he had been a journalist. First he had been a painter, then he made a living writing for Hungarian newspapers. And then he took up photography."

HM looking at some of his work

Bijou was this fantastic-looking creature, filthy and scaly. Her skin was caked with dirt, her eyes were heavily black, her fingernails were filthy, everything about her was filthy. But she had those marvelous big eyes and she read your fortune. . . . She was a character.

Brassaï and Picasso

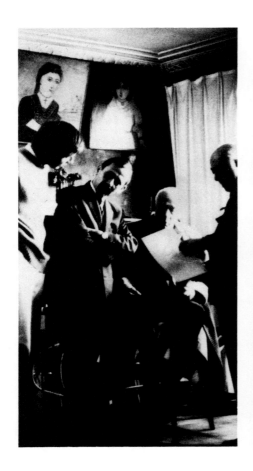

"Bijou" by Brassaï.

Brassaï – "the Eyes of Paris"

Scenes of Paris

Paris — Streets and Places

Grand Hôtel de la France — rue Bonaparte
Cafés — Dôme, Select, Rotonde, Coupole — Montparnasse
Cafés — Zeyer and Bouquet d'Alésia — at Carrefour d'Alésia
The rue de la Gaîté (and Café de la Liberté at corner of Blvd. Edgar Quinet)
The Villa Seurat (Boris' place) "Villa Borghese"
The Canal St. Martin — leading to Jean Jaurès district
Cinéma Vanves (called "Splendide" in book) — rue de Vanves (name changed now)
The Palais Royal and Jardin des Tuileries
Jardin du Luxembourg
The American Express — rue Scribe
Place St. Sulpice — and Restaurant des Gourmets — rue des Canettes
The Flea Market (?)
The Gare St. Lazare (rush hour) — Salle des Pas Perdus
Rue du Château — railroad bridge (Gare Montparnasse)
Walls and kiosks with posters for Cinzano, amer Picon, zigzag, Dubonnet, etc.
Hôtel des États-Unis — Blvd. Montparnasse
The rue de Buci — Hôtel de la Louisiane (Carco, Sartre, Cossery, Beauvoir....)
Rue de l'Échaudé (whorehouses — passed thru every night on way to work)
Square de Furstemberg
Rue St. Denis, Faubourg du Temple) — Life selling!
Cité Nortier (near Place du Combat) — Life selling!
Blvd. Beaumarchais — rue Pasteur-Wagner + rue Amelot (Germaine) (Café de l'Éléphant)
The Bal Nègre — rue Blomet
The Bal on rue Fontaine
The Cirque Medrano
The rue Amélie — one of my favorites (Hôtel Pretty)
Rue Mouffetard (food) — Place Contrescarpe (Clochards) — Rues des Patriarches
Rue de Bret-...il — Place Vauban — Les Invalides (Napoleon)
The Folies-Bergère (Serge + antiseptics) — Café des Artistes
Gaumont Palace — Place Clichy — Café Wepler (Red light — girl with wooden leg)
(running counter on rue d'Alésia around corner)
Rue des Hôtel — balcony with red signs
Rue Froidevaux — horses clip-clop going to slaughterhouse
Street paralleling cemetery Montparnasse — Sinister at night (Schwartz)
Rue Lafayette — Montmartre's ...ist — newspaper office!
Gidotte's Pigtrot in rear — where mirrors + pumps etc
The Bal Tabarin — the Can-Can! (or the moulin Rouge)
The House of all nations (Prince Edward) — ?
Miss Hamilton's Institut (rue Laferrière — off rue Fontaine(?) (Hindus)
Blvd. de la Chapelle (near Aubervilliers) — les vieilles grandeurs! (Under metro)
Rue du Faubourg Montmartre
The Pont des Arts (at 3 A.M.)
The Rue Laffitte (2 churches framed above)
The Sacre Coeur and Place du Tertre — Montmartre
Rue St. Séverin + St. Médard — Girodias' neighborhood (crabs + Gradls)
Place des Vosges + St. Paul quartier — Rue des Rosiers (Jewish)
Île St. Louis (Tana + Baudelaire)
Église Ste. Clothilde (de Nerval — suicide — ?)
Russian church — near Villette (Russian marriage — Olga + Anatole)
Walk to + from Newspaper — evening + early morning
Place de l'Entrepôt (Jean Cocteau)
The Rue Lhomond — Place Lucien Herr
Pension Orfila — rue d'Assas (Strindberg — Jadrine) — looking at S's room!
Hôtel du Tombeau des Lapins — and other queer names! (Montparnasse)
Place Violet + Passage des Thermopyles
Abattoir Hippophagiques — rue des Périchaux (Vaugirard)

(2.) Paris — Streets and Places

Les Halles and surrounding streets and bars — rue Quincampoix, Rambuteau, etc. (Whores, Bars, Restaurants)
Rue Broca (under viaduct)
Impasse Satan
Le Mosquée — Sign re Syphilis (Gouttes militaires — ghost)
The Sphinx — Blvd. Montparnasse
Rue de la Lune — Grands Blvds. (shops there + notkels)
Place Nationale, Place des Peupliers, Place Paul Verlaine, rue du Château des Rentiers (13e arr.)
Place d'Italie (picturesque)
Porte d'Orléans (last talk with Cadrans at hotel terrace!)
Rue St. Apolline — Kruger's brothel there
Rue Grégoire la Tour — Brassaï's brothel — card playing
The Café Boudon — Montmartre (rue Fontaine) (from 5 to 7)
Little bars + restaurants at top of Montmartre (from 5 to 7)
Place Dupleix — Cavalry Barracks, Russian church, Eiffel Tower
Hôtel Princesse (near St. Germain) — Anna +? (phooo — Smoke gets in your eyes)
Rond-Point des Champs Élysées — different kind of whores (5 - 7)
Brick tops (Montparnasse) — Jimmy's Bar — rue Huyghens — Montparnasse
Place d'Aligre
Le Monocle and le Fétiche (Lesbian joints) — rue d'Odessa (!)

by Brassaï

À ce point ici, c'est le moment de demander; où êtes-vous avec votre manuscrit?

Where is he now? I'm asking. He's writing a book, you know, like he did for Picasso, he's writing one, I've never seen any of it.

Écoutez. Je vais vous lire ici. Très peu, hein?

À huit heures et demie, à l'hôtel Mont Fleuri, sur la colline de Californie, non loin de la villa de Picasso, à la réception le concierge me dit, "Monsieur Miller est très fatigué. Jusqu'à l'heure du déjeuner il a inderdit tout coup de téléphone, toute visite." "Monsieur Miller m'attends ce matin," lui dis-je, "et je vous prie de m'annoncer avec son petit dejeuner."

Pendant que je passe, j'entends la voix d'un homme qui à côté de moi discute avec le concièrge de l'hôtel. "Mais non, pas une planche a repasser, ni une planche en pin—une simple planche en bois blanc, juste assez large pour que je puisse me coucher dessus, je n'ai jamais pu dormir dans un lit, mais sur une planche au pied du lit." Comme l'homme a un regeux accent espagnol, le concierge le comprend avec difficulté. Mais moi, sachant qu'à l'hôtel l'Aiglon à Paris, sur le boulevard Raspail, ce singulier client dormait déjà sur une planche en bois, je devine aussitôt, bien que je ne le connaisse pas personnellement, qu'il ne peut s'agir que du metteur en scène Luis Bunuel. . . .

Oui, c'est vrai que je l'ai rencontré.

L'homme d'une trentaine d'années, à ses côtés, sans doute son fils Juan-Luis, qui comme assistant travaille avec lui. Ce que le gérant du Mont Fleuri ignore, c'est que Bunuel, dans ce même hôtel l'Aiglon, préferait à faire sa cuisine dans sa chambre, et que les odeurs fortement parfumés empestaient les couloirs de l'hôtel et incommodaient les clients. "Monsieur Miller vous prie de monter," m'annonce le concierge, au milieu d'une grande en bout de paton.

Oui, oui. . . . inondée de lumière, entourée d'une térrasse surplombant un parc magnifique de palmiers qui me rappellent Rio, Henry est en train de prendre son petit déjeuner.

"Je suis très touché que vous soyez dérangé pour cette histoire d'émission, vous m'aiderez beaucoup souvenir."

"Comment c'est passé le voyage?" "Je n'ai pas été très heureux à Rome, je n'aime pas cette ville, peut être tombé à l'inverse; nous les voyons en tauge, les bras nus. Je les ai toujours imaginé vivant sous un climat chaud africain. Comment les romains pouvaient-ils se promener ici, sans pardessus, sans imperméable, sans pullover, sans gants, sans chaussettes de laines."

He translated for my benifit, knowing that I had a hard time keeping up with his French.

"Listen, I'll read it to you here—just a short bit, OK?"

These few paragraphs describe an incident when Brassaï, visiting Henry unexpectedly at the Hotel Mont Fleuri, witnessed the arrival of the eccentric—and very famous—motion-picture director, Luis Bunuel.

I wrote about it here, but I didn't want to tell you that this hotel was the Gestapo. They brought people here to torture them ... down there, in your room. I didn't dare tell you, because I didn't want you to be affected by it.

Henry
Brassaï
HM:
Brassaï
HM:

Brassaï
HM:

But deep down, you are actually the world's first hippie.

Brassaï
HM:
Brassaï
HM:

Dissolve to HM and
Beauford Delaney;
in Delaney's studio

Beauford Delaney

Jesus, that's another place. You've missed all this Bob, but I guess that this was where he meets me at a marvelous hotel where I was put up, when I was with a girl.

J'ai écris ici, je ne voulais pas vous dire, mais je savais que cet hôtel était le Gestapo.

Oui, vraiment?

L'hôtel le Mont Fleuri était le Gestapo. On y amenait tous les gens et on torturait les gens. Là-bas, dans votre chambre. Je n'osais pas vous le dire parce-que je ne voulais pas que vous soyez impressionné par cette chose.

Oui.

Mais on m'a dit, n'est-ce pas, j'ai écrit ça. Vraiment.

Vous êtes sur de ce que vous dites?

Absolument.

Oui?

Oui, oui, comme il y avait Gestapo, à la Côte d'Azur, c'était le Gestapo.

Ai, ai, ai, ai, ai.

A beautiful hotel, Oh, my, wonderful.

Afterwards, some time later, I go back to that hotel with another girl, I think, I don't remember, and I stay there a few days. I know it's expensive, too expensive for me. I stay three, four days, and when I go to pay my bill, the hotel manager says to me: *"C'est payé."* Le *monsieur, qui est le propriétaire, c'est un bancaire. Oui, il a le plaisir.*

Ah, vous n'avez rien à payer?

Non, hm.

Mais vous êtes, au fond, vous êtes l'origine des hippies—beatniks?

On dit ça, oui, comme si je suis responsable (laughter). . . .

Why don't you come back? I'll make a new painting of you.

Do you know you did one of me one time in New York? I had a slide made of it. There it is . . . and that's also in those bright colors—a sort of a halo around me almost I felt.

By the way, look around, anything you might see here, anything at all that you like, you can have. Don't say no to it, take your time.

And what's that over there?

Marian Anderson. . . .

I suppose it was no accident that being an admirer of the work of Paul Klee, I finally, I finally became good friends with a painter who could rightly be called his twin soul. I mean Hans Reichel, whom I got to know soon after my arrival in Paris. If I were limited to knowing only one artist in a lifetime, one who would enable me to understand the meaning and the purpose of art, I would probably say give me Hans Reichel. Reichel was of the damned, a true poet *maudit*, wedded to his art, he lived it day by day. He lived for nothing else. It was his misfortune to paint in the manner that reminded someone of Paul Klee. "How can I help it," he once said to me, "if we see the world through the same eyes?"

Ah, isn't it like entering a little chapel here? There's something holy about it. Reichel's world was a limited one. It comprised of a few, very few, devoted friends. In truth, he hardly ever left the precincts of the 14th Aron, where he lived. For him it was sufficient to take a stroll through the Parc Mont Souris and the Luxembourg Gardens. He had friends there whom he visited regularly—the birds, the plants, the fishes, the squirrels. He talked to them and they answered him. A small world perhaps, but a full and rewarding one.

Gregory Michonze—one of the first painters I met in Paris. A man thoroughly dedicated to his work.

Tell me about your life.

You know what I do; I paint pictures, that's all. I paint pictures.

And religiously.

I have tried to continue a tradition. Just. And I am not puzzling about doing anything new at all.

You know the one painter I like the most after all these years? I look at his work, is Bonnard.

Bonnard is tremendous.

By the way, why don't you pull out something of yours that you like, something new?

A lot of pictures in the making. I'm doing a lot of things on paper.

On paper, with oils?

Oh yes, I sell the pictures unfinished. Always my clients buy from me unfinished work; they pay me, and I finish the painting.

Dissolve to photo of
Hans Reichel and int. of
Reichel's studio

Paris studio of Gregory Michonze
and some of his work

Beauford Delaney's Paris studio.

*Beauford Delaney and H.M.
outside Delaney's studio
Paris*

Portrait of Henry Miller by
Beauford Delaney

Of all the artists I have been privileged to associate with throughout my long life I could hardly have known four individuals more different from one another in so many ways than Reichel, Brassaï, Michonze and Delaney. Yet they all had one thing in common, a virtue usually possessed only by the saints — I mean patience. And by patience I mean the everlasting courage to persist in the path one has chosen despite all obstacles.

All through modern times it seems to be expected of the artist that he be a martyr, first as a failure, then as a success. One doesn't know which heaven or which hell is preferable. One has no choice.

I regard myself as extremely fortunate to have been a friend of these remarkable individuals, to have been inspired and fortified by their example during the Paris years when I too was struggling to be born.

I feel honored to be a humble participant in this exhibition of their work.

Henry Miller
December, 1971

by Gregory Michonze

by Hans Reichel

Gregory Michonze

You know why I mention Isaac Bashevis Singer, because your work reminds me so much of his writing. It's, like, inexhaustible in this theme.

Animal, horse, anything. Ask me what I have in my head; I have nothing. All my brains go into my fingers. My brain is in my fingers. I have a hell of a time thinking of a title of a picture. So I'm just the same as an abstractionist. The only difference is I'm fearfully faithful to life.

Is it any wonder that there are so many poet-painters in France? Wherever the eye falls there is color, irregularity, whimsey, individuality, together with all the evidences of old age and youth, the patina of life lived. Even in the simple matter of dress there is a marked lack of uniformity. As for the shops, they are infinite in variety, as variegated as the proprieters themselves. As for the street itself, there one can still see the old and the bent, the crippled, the half-witted, the *mutilés de la guerre*, the genuinely demented, the beggars and tramps,

the drunkards, pitched against the plenum of colorful delapidated walls. Windows of every size and description. Shaded allées, cathedrals. Notre Dame rises tomblike out of the waters. Hideous and charming monuments, strident posters and billboards, chimney pots and black roofs, pale rose and siena roofs, vegetables piled sky-high and arranged like gems, mangy cats, sad looking curs, everything imaginable and often the unimaginable, all bizarre and nostalgic, thoroughly off-beat. A mélange or stew that never fails to whet the appetite of a poet or painter.

I think when you suffer somewhere and you can't escape, you begin to accept the situation and then you find marvelous things in it. So in the midst of my poverty and suffering and all that, I really discovered Paris, and the true French spirit and everything. And got to love it. Of course that's a hard thing to understand—how can you enjoy being right down to the very bottom? And that's the most important thing that ever happened to me—to be without anything, no crutch of any kind. Cut off completely from any help, and to have to find it every day, this help to live from day to day. This is a very good thing, you know. You suffer, sure. You're miserable. But it's so interesting, it's so fascinating, you're so thoroughly alive, when you do that. You're living then with your instincts like an animal, and that's a great thing for us overcivilized people. To know again how to live like a bird of prey or, you know, an animal, wolfing every meal; and begging, and being humiliated, accepting it, being pushed down and then bouncing back up again; each day is a miracle that you get through, do you see. This is a very wonderful thing.

Paris scenes

You'd think that an author has definite ideas and plans and all that; well he does in a slight way. But you write in order to find out what you're writing about, who you are and why, and what for. It's a voyage of discovery. You begin with all your charts and plans and compasses and everything, it's a good thing, you get where you want to go. But the object of writing is to not know where you're going. My hatreds and rebellions against the society that we live in, especially our American society, made me choose foul language, not to shock them so much as because I am disturbed and angry and so on. So all I can say is shit fuck piss and all that. Do you know what I mean. Get it out, spill it on them, you know.

Dissolve to scene at table in Paris apartment with HM, Durrell, and Alfred Perlès

I had two especially good boon companions who are still alive, still writing, and we are still writing to one another. That's Lawrence Durrell—and Alfred Perlès, whom I call Alf always . . . my boon companion throughout the ten-year's stay in Paris—author of a number of books in French, German, and English—and who saved my life when I was on the point of returning to America or committing suicide.

Remember the very first evening at the Dôme? You were sitting there in back of a big pile of dishes. There was a pile that high of courses which you couldn't pay for, remember? I don't know if you had a room or not, but at that point I invited you to come to my hotel in the Hotel Central . . .

Night scenes of Paris hotels and Hotel Central

Well, then you proposed that I share that little room up there in that hell of a place. You used to take me home and . . .

Perlès

I worked on the night shift, you see, and you could sneak in at night . . .

HM:

I used to tread softly, like Smerdyakov, in your footsteps so that it would sound like one person, and then you would say to the night porter, "Perlès," and I was marching slowly behind you, whispering. Do you remember? And then you used to leave money on the mantelpiece so that at least I could have my croissant and coffee in the morning. You didn't leave enough for lunch because you didn't have any money. Then began my day, looking for lunch and looking for dinner.

Scenes of Paris

I remember with such pleasure my early days in Paris, when I walked the streets with an empty belly, stopping every few yards to gaze at the paintings, sketches, books, objects d'art displayed in the shop windows. Bread . . . prime symbol. Americans don't care about good bread. Dying of inanition, they go on eating bread without substance, without flavor, without vitamins, without life. The very core of life is contaminated. Think of French bread, so many varieties of bread, all

French bread

wonderful: *la baguette de fusil, le pain de seigle, le pain de fantasiê, le pain de campagne, le pain de mie,* and not the least of all, *le croissant.*

Clichy was a marvelous workingman's quarter with a Communist mayor. Here Perlès and I finally settled in, after a hand-to-mouth existence, hotel to hotel, and spent almost two years writing, playing, horsing around. The day that we landed in that place, do you remember, the first place that we could really call our own, we arrived there in the late afternoon . . .

P. . . . We came with all our luggage, everything ready, ready to move in, and then we looked at the wall. . . . Do you remember the wall? Crawling with bedbugs, do you remember that? They were coming down like soldiers . . .

M: I lived two or three years in Clichy. I came here the first time in 1928. I can see this place going on for another hundred years—what's to stop it? Isn't it nice? What's to hinder? They make more transformations: another kind of lighting, some other kind of *demimondaine* instead of *prostituée.* (*Laugh.*)

(*At Café Wepler, Clichy*) *If, as I've thought, his writing is unimaginable without his Brooklyn accent, his French is unthinkable without his Brooklyn accent (we gave some serious thought to putting on English subtitles for the groundlings; but apart from the expense, and the distraction from the image that sub-titles forces on the viewer, it seemed absurd that one couldn't understand his primer, almost sign-language French).*

.;. . I'm sitting over in the corner reading . . . what am I reading? *Je lis Élie Faure, je crois, et après quelques, n'est-ce pas,* how do I say and I thought she signaled, *elle a signé,* "Come over to my table." But she meant, "I'll see you outside." *Elle veut dire, "Àpres, n'est-ce pas? en dehors."* And she was embarrassed. She didn't want to be thought of as a *demimondaine.* And then she says, "*Vous êtes Américain?*" "*Oui.*" "*Qu'est-ce que vous lisez? Français?*" "*Oui.*" *Elle regarde comme ça, et finalement, elle dit: "Il n'est pas français."*

And don't you remember too, that night the girls were leaving—they weren't exactly girls—and they wanted money, and none of us ever had money, and you had a checkbook from an account that didn't exist, and you were writing a check and handing it to the girl in the bathtub. And she said, What! that piece of paper? What'll I do with that? That's no good.

Pendant que nous vivons en Anatole France, Fred had—how do you say, had, *trouvé une jeune fille, 14 ou 15 . . .* she was wandering in the streets. *Perdu!* He rescued her, brought her home—to live—with us!

Dissolve to scenes
of Clichy

Ext. Café Wepler
in Clichy

Int. café; MCU
HM at table

Perlès

Après quelques semaines, on frappe à la porte, . . . et voilà . . hunh, . . . *la mère et le père. Et très cultivés, très respectable. Et d'abord, le monsieur dit: "C'est très grave, n'est-ce pas? Elle est une mineure."* Minor—*c'est la prison. Pendant qu'il parle à Fred, il voit le bibliothèque*—the library, a very very little library—and he sees Goethe, . . . who else? . . . Keyserling. . . . *"Vous êtes quelqu'un qui lisez des bons livres, vous êtes cultivé; comment est-ce que vous pouvez commettre un crime?" Et, finalement, monsieur entends que je tappe à la machine et Fred dit: "Excusez-moi, je vais vous presenter mon ami, Henri Miller. Henri Miller est de rien dire, mais j'avais une figure assez impressionable et sérieuse, et il dit: "Qu'est-ce qu'il ecrit, le monsieur?" Et Fred lui dit: "La philosophie, la métaphysique, oui, comme un guru. Et, comme ça, Fred est exonéré. "Mais," le monsieur dit, "attention! Ne répétez pas, n'est-ce pas? Si ma fille reviendra encore un fois—la prison."* It was wonderful.

Clichy was a happy period. We had a flat—a kitchen and two bedrooms—borrowed the money from some wealthy woman. . . . Bedbugs crawling up and down the walls; we made them fumigate. We worked on the Chicago *Tribune* as proofreaders. We'd get up around noon every day, then have breakfast—lunch—write a bit, and then go for a spin on the bikes. Then we ate before going to work, at a workingman's restaurant. The meals were very cheap—ten francs. The ordinary American tourist would spend 18 to 30 francs and think he was eating reasonably. We'd see the same people in these places every night—curious people—we never knew them intimately, but always greeted them. There was never an intrusion on your privacy.

Across the street was a hotel. On a rainy night two or three girls would stand with umbrellas—strange and lovely sight—seemingly so respectable, soliciting. That all seemed to wash in with the food.

I wrote *Black Spring* and worked on a book on Lawrence that I never finished. I was writing *Capricorn*. We would have champagne before starting out in the evening and we ate at the cafe where all the prostitutes came in with their pimps—their *maqueraux*—and we all sat at the same table until five in the morning. We worked from 8 PM to 2 AM.

On the plan for The World of D. H. Lawrence.

Let me tell you about that. . . . I got so involved, I couldn't get him (Lawrence) off my mind. It became an obsession: I read all his books, and I read all about him. . . . and I used to beg the powers that be—raising my hands in prayer—stop dictating to me. But I'd made these big charts . . . then I got lost in the forest: I was so mixed up that I started contradicting myself . . . and I decided to forget the whole damned thing. It was the only failure I ever had, y'know; the only book I never finished, you might say.

Letter from the Paris edition of the Chicago Tribune, firing H.M.

LA VIE DE BOHÈME
(As Lived on the Left Bank)

BY WAMBLY BALD

Even in this barren age with its economic problems, romance is just around the corner. Indeed, adventure waits at night in the dark streets of Paris.

Night before last all the stars were out and I was walking very slowly to appreciate their beauty. Occasionally a painted smile tried to block my way, but I wandered on and on under the big stars. And looking at a full moon often gives me an emotion.

Near the shadows of the Louvre a lone figure began to follow me and tapped me on the shoulder after a short chase. He was dressed in corduroy, a gray jacket and thick spectacles. His hat was carelessly jammed on one side of his head and the uncovered side was quite bald. It was Henry Miller, the novelist.

"Hello," I said. We talked about this and that and smoked a few cigarettes. Then I said:

"Where are you going?"

He replied, "Nowhere in particular."

That's just like Miller. He is never definite. Miller has been out of a job for some time and he hasn't a cent. But he's lucky. He has friends. They always take care of him.

A couple of days ago he woke up on a bench outside the Closerie des Lilas. The only thing that bothered him, he said, was that he didn't have a toothbrush. "Being on the bum is all right if you can clean your teeth occasionally — say, every third day. Otherwise you feel bad."

But he doesn't worry. His friends are always backing him up. The other day he met Kann the sculptor, who has just landed a fat contract from America. They dined at Ciro's. During the meal Miller reached in his pocket for a handkerchief and pulled out a pair of socks. At Ciro's! In the evening he met another friend, Joe Chock. Joe has just broken into Broadway with a burlesque on heaven. It's a radio play. The hero goes around through five acts with a microphone concealed in his caleçons. Miller likes friend Joe because the latter drinks champagne and smokes Coronas. Miller showed me a few of the butts he had collected. Succulent snipes. He smokes only the best butts when he is with Joe.

A good word is *esprit*. I told him that. "You have *esprit*," I said, lighting his cigar butt. Then he said:

"Can you give me an alarm clock?"

"What for?"

"Well, you see, Joe,"—(he always calls me Joe. He calls everybody Joe.)—"I

Henry Val Miller

am having such a good time that I hate to miss any of it. I like to get up early to enjoy every available hour."

Suddenly Miller staggered and fell back against the wall of a building. "What's the matter," I said. His voice was frail and I could read between the lines of his face.

"What you need is food," I said, reaching in my pockets. "I'm your friend, too. Get yourself some food." I said, and handed him a franc. Montparnasse is that way.

(last column)

sketch done by Halazy in de la Liberté des Éditions "Edgar" on

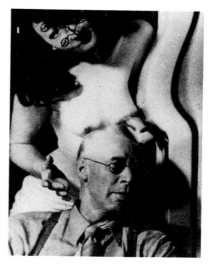

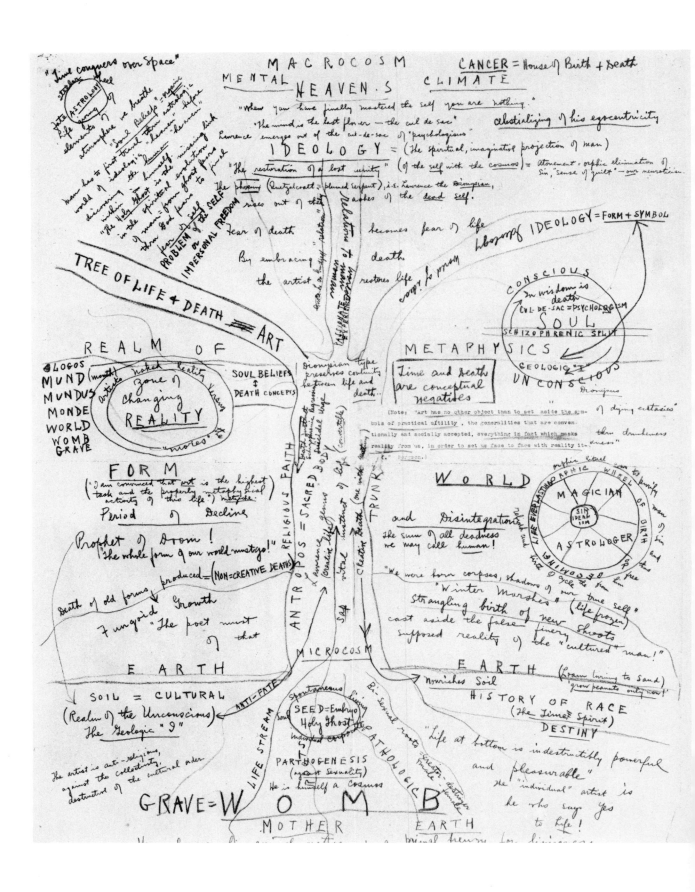

Anaïs Nin

HM

Dissolve to photo of
night scene in street
with pissoires

A lot of this came about from knowing Otto Rank and getting filled up on all his works, *The Trauma of Birth, Art and Artists*—all those books.

"You were interested in Rank because of his interest in history, art and anthropology; you weren't interested in him as an analyst, but in his knowledge."

Right, right; and in his failure as a human being, don't y'know—it was so tragic . . .

I do not find it strange that America placed a urinal in the middle of the Paris exhibit in Chicago. I think it belongs there, and I think it a tribute that the French should be proud of. How is a Frenchman to know that what impresses the American in looking at a *pissotiere* or a *vespasienne*, or whatever you call it, is the fact that he's in the midst of a people who admit to the necessity of peeing now and then, and who know also that to piss one has to use a pisser. I am a man who pisses largely and frequently, which they say is a sign of great mental activity. One likes to piss in sunlight among human beings who stand and smile down at you. Standing behind a tin strip and looking out on the throng with that contented, easy, vacant smile, that long reminiscent pleasurable look, is a good thing. How many times have I stood thus in this smiling gracious world, the sun splashing over me and the birds twittering crazily, and found a woman looking down at me from an open window. Standing thus with heart and bly and bladder open, I seem to recall every urinal I ever stepped into. To relieve a full bladder is one of the great human joys.

Anatole France, Chichy
Dear Emil,

Letter to Emil

Letter to Emil;
dissolve to HM in studio
painting a watercolor

It doesn't go so easily, the watercolor business. This one is a sample of what I can turn out, a sample of my inability to make headway. I just must get some first-hand knowledge. A little idea of the craft, something besides inspiration and enthusiasm. I'm disgusted for the moment. Night before in despair, doubts, failure, old age. Morning comes, the bowels move, the earth groans. I don't think about any single thing, but about all things at once. I want to show the world

that not all the great surrealists are dead. I want a classic purity, where dung is dung, and angels are angels. The Bible à la King James, for example; the glorious death-dealing Bible created when the English language was in flower, when a vocabulary of 20,000 words sufficed to build a monument for all time.

I want a classic purity, where dung is dung and angels are angels. The Bible a la King James, for example. Not the Bible of Wycliffe, not the

Vulgate, not the Greek, not the Hebrew, but the glorious, death-dealing Bible that was created when the English language was in flower, when a vocabulary of twenty thousand words sufficed to build a monument for all time. A Bible written in Svenska or Tegalic, a Bible for the Hottentots or the Chinese, a Bible that has to meander through the trickling sands of French is no Bible—it is a counterfeit and a fraud. The King James Version was created by a race of bone-crushers. It revives the primitive mysteries, revives rape, murder, incest, revives epilepsy, sadism, megalomania, revives demons, angels, dragons, leviathans, revives magic, exorcism, contagion, incantation, revives fratricide, regicide, patricide, suicides, revives hypnotism, anarchism, somnambulism, revives the song, the dance, the act, revives the mantic, the ehthonian, the arcane, the mysterious, revived the power, the evil and the glory that is God. All brought into the open on a colossal scale, and so salted and spiced that it will last until the next Ice Age.

A classic purity, then—and to hell with the Post Office authorities!

In my world people will piss warm and drink cold, people will piss and shit and fuck and curse and groan and die and are sent to heaven and come back again in the flesh and hang on a cross in the shop window. Well here I am and I'm showing them my ass. I can write and I will write and nobody will deny me. I will write what no man dares to say and they can take it or leave it, and I think they will take it.

Dissolve to street and Villa Seurat with HM and wife

After Clichy I moved to the Villa Seurat where I had a studio and some real comforts. The street itself is famous for harboring many famous painters, sculptors, musicians. Dali had a house on the corner . . . Lurçat, Gromaire. . . . And after Fraenkel left Soutine moved in. Here I finished the third or fourth revisions revision of *Tropic of Cancer*, wrote *Tropic of Capricorn*, *Man and the White Phagocyte*, *Aller Retour N.Y.*, finished *Black Spring* and began the *Hamlet Letters* with Michael Fraenkel.

Cover of Tropic of Cancer

But, at any rate, I found my voice in Paris, and I wrote that book which started all the trouble and success at the same time, and that was the *Tropic of Cancer*.

Dissolve to HM at studio desk

I suppose one could liken *The Tropic of Cancer* to the volcano's eruption, to the breaking of the crust. (Only, let me say it as knows, it was such a feeble eruption compared to those imaginary streetwalking ones I had every day, inwardly, walking to and from my father's shop!)

SELBSTPORTRAIT FÜR CHARLIE CHAPLIN, 1919   Lithographie

If I had only had this guy
to illustrate "Tropic of Cancer"

Property of
Henry V. Miller
4 Ave. Anatole France
Clichy (Seine) – France.

"Tropic of ~~Capricorn~~ Cancer"

by

Anonymous

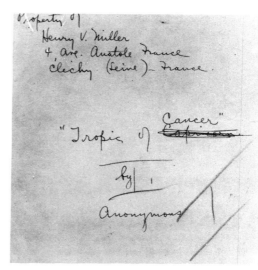

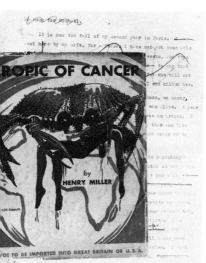

I asked him whether it was signed "Anonyme" because he feared censorship. "Not at all; at the time we were discussing the role of the artist, whether he was a creator or merely an anonymous, if sensitive, transmitter."

You know I spent many a sleepless night thinking of titles. Oh I had hundreds of titles. And I don't remember how I stumbled on *Tropic of Cancer*. I can't—yes, I remember now, it's coming back. I was much interested then—this was in Paris—I was much interested then in Chinese philosophy and in numbers and I had read that great great book—what Keyserling called the greatest, the most famous. . . .

I Ching.

Now then, how does it come? Oh yes, then I begin to understand that the crab in China is an important symbol for the reason that it can move in any direction. Backwards, forwards, and sideways, and that idea intrigued me very much. Then also I thought it's a cancerous world I'm dealing with, do you see. Yeah, I remember. But it was a great find, it was a great title wasn't it. It proved to be. Generally speaking all my titles are good.

I remember *Tropic of Capricorn*, it began with the *Ovarian Trolley*. And I intended to write two or three volumes under the title *Capricorn*. And then I forgot. There was an interruption and I forgot what I was going to do.

LP: You forgot because you didn't make a list. My God if I laid all the lists you made end to end in this file, you'd have a. . . .

HM: What is that now, one of those Paris notebooks?

LP: Yeah, Paris. I don't know when you ever got time to write because you were so busy making those lists.

Lawrence Powell wasn't in Paris at the time, but Henry's lists were ongoing...

Dissolve to HM and Lawrence Durrell seated in drawing room at LD's home in Provence

Lawrence Durrell, author of the *Alexandria Quartet* and other well-known books, came to see me in Paris at about the age of twenty-three or four as a young writer and remained an everlasting friend.

I can always see you as the very young man who knocked on my door at the Villa Seurat. You came in, you peeked in, you put your head in the door, the crack, I can see you now, you know. I grabbed you and hugged you and you always remained to me like that. As you get to be 70 years old and I'm 95 or 100, I'll still think of you as that. . . .

I was particularly struck by his greeting, because after hugging me, he said, "Let me take a look at you." Then he pulls up my trouser leg and says, "Christ, you're built like a tree." A most original way of being greeted by the *cher maître*.

My first impression was he was like a boxer, he wasn't exactly a bantam, he was heavier than that, yet he was light, but he had that lightfooted quality, agility and everything, a little bit of pugnacity, which he still has, in his chin.

From dealing with publishers.

Yes, . . . he always struck me as a boxer.

(Nîmes Story) While we were visiting Durrell in Provence, we took in some of Henry's favorite places there—Aigues-Mortes Arles, and Nîmes (Van Gogh and Delteil country) and Nîmes. After a great luncheon at the Hotel de France across from the Nîmes Amphitheatre, we entered the arena; and, at its center, Henry and Larry paused to talk. With his customary dash, Larry set the scene; putting the thumbs of his outspread hands into his ears, he lowered his head and charged at Henry. Henry took the cue, stretched erect, put his cane over his extended arm and delivered the coup de grace*—just before which, I heard the tell-tale clicks of the film running out. Now this was too good to miss: I waited and debated. I dilly-dallied and deliberated: I had not broken the ground rules (of not asking Henry to do anything, certainly not repeating anything). But this was just too good—and by now, surely, I was intimate and secure enough to dare. . . . So I leaned into the "scene," excusing my interruption, "Gentlemen, would you mind doing that once more, pretty please" (surely, Baylis had reloaded the camera by now): and without a moment's by your leave, they obliged. And no camera sound reached me until Henry had finished his* coup de grace*. I could have killed Baylis—but he was obviously unwell: perhaps the luncheon was over-rich for his mid-Western stomach since he almost killed himself by falling off the top of the ampitheatre, where he had climbed to get the establishing shot. I simply could not ask them to do it again—three strikes and you're out—knowing full well that it would haunt me for the rest of my life.*

It was a tremendous pleasure to get out into the provinces. Every province in France is extremely interesting, colorful, a nation unto itself.

Mountaineers, land people, wine country which makes for some kind of happiness. And it's an authentic sort of country, like a cultural country where the people live close to or on the land, have a kind of bone structure.

It was there that I found people who were lazy, and who knew how to talk and how to live. How to do nothing. And it was a great relief after the northern spirit of France.

Dissolve to HM and Durrell in Roman amphitheater at Nîmes

Lawrence Durrell and HM walking

Lawrence Durrell

Alfred Perlès a young man.

In the Luxembourg Gardens:
Snyder, Miller, Glusko,
Durrell.

HM and Lawrence Durrell

Provence

Henry and Lawrence Durrell at the amphitheatre in Nimes.

Dissolve to bridge in Provence; HM, his wife, and Durrell walking in streets of Sommières

L.D.

It's architecturally very beautiful. It's French, which means that the eating is quite better than anywhere else in the world. There's contentment in the belly.

I much prefer to live down there than to live in Paris, or any other city of France.

There's a metaphysical uneasiness which is creative. You know I have something very urgent I wanted to discuss with you. I couldn't sleep last night and I took that book about suicides up to bed with me and I remembered all our conversations about Njinsky's madness and so on and so forth, and I wondered if suicide, or the desire for it is a young man's feeling or an elderly man's. Does one feel more and more suicidal or less and less suicidal as one goes on? I was more at twenty and less now at fifty. How did it work with you?

HM:

That's the same, same with me, except now and then I could say there are little interludes—*ça revient*—and it's terrible when it occurs later in life, the desire to commit suicide. But it doesn't last as long. You see when you're younger, you could have this feeling, and it could go on for weeks at a time, months, do you know what I mean. You're desperate, and what not. Everything is black. Later in life, it comes quick, sudden like, and for no reason. It seems to me it also passes more quickly, or that's my feeling.

L.D.

Did you ever choose a method?

HM:

Yes, I had several methods. Drowning was one. I tried that one. And I tried taking the pill. I had a friend, a doctor, who gave me a pill to commit suicide. And to make sure it would work I opened up the window wide. It was winter, the snow came in. I layed naked on the bed. He must have really given me a sleeping pill. I thought he really gave me something to kill me. I took it, I went to sleep immediately. I woke up, the snow was on me, and I didn't even have a cough.

HM and Anaïs Nin in room at Anaïs's home

And, of course, there was a third, perhaps more important friend than the other two of them in my life, and that was Anaïs Nin—*une être étoilique*—author of the now famous *Diary*, an inspiration and a protectress of so many striving artists including yours truly, Henry Miller.

Dissolve to photos of Louveciennes and Anaïs Nin

Anaïs had a home at Louveciennes in an old village about an hour distant from Paris by bicycle. Beautiful home on what was formerly the estate of Marie Antoinette. It was a charming place.

And you gave me great help I remember because you used to go over my early scripts and say, "Look, don't put all that in. It isn't necessary." You used to have to fight me about it because I thought it

Anaïs Nin and
Louveciennes.

A.N.

LS: Anaïs Nin ascending
stairs of Bradbury building
in Los Angeles. Dissolve
to 2-shot AN and HM
seated in gárden

HM:

A.N.

HM:

A.N.

HM:

was important. I thought everything was important. Now you know, if I could, if I had the power, I would reduce everything, I would write the smallest books if I could. I appreciate them you know.

But you turned out to be right, because everybody was more worried about what I left out than what I put in.

I never believed what they say that the obsession that Fraenkel and Lowenfels, the obsession of death that they had, that you shared that, and I said no, I didn't think you ever. . . . You played with them and their terminology, if you like, but you never were very concerned about death, about destruction, about the destruction of the world. . . .

But what they were talking about really, Anaïs, was death in life, which so many people have—death in life, don't you know.

But you don't know anything about that.

No, but I become more aware all the time.

That there are people who are dead in life.

Oh yes, and that's the only death, that's the real death. Not this death when you depart the body, but being dead while you are alive, that's the real death. I'll tell you one thing. You got into this thing through psychoanalysis; from your talk (Eduardo's, everybody talks about dreams) I began to dream very heavily, violently, every night. And then I learned how to wake up without losing the dream. This is an art and a discipline, and I've discovered that. I've lost it again, but I can do it if I want. You learn how to wake up. You don't wake up, you don't open your eyes wide right away, and you wake up, and you know you've been dreaming when you wake up, and you close your eyes slowly again, and you go back onto that last thread, and you go back into the labyrinth, trace it back, do you see. And when I get it all down I go in my pajamas to the typewriter and record it. And not only record the dream, but all the associations that came with it.

Reading from the
Colossus of Maroussi :

After ten years in Paris, just before war was declared, I accepted Lawrence Durell's invitation to go to his place in Corfu, Greece, where I spend a few marvelous months, again, perhaps, the high peak of my life. When I returned from Greece, I immediately sat down and wrote the *Colussus of Maroussi*, which I still think is my best book.

Close-up :
Henry Miller's
face. Voice over

It is the morning of the first day of the great peace. The peace of the heart which comes with surrender. I never knew the meaning of peace until I arrived at Epidauris. Like everyone I had used the word all my

life without once realizing that I was using a counterfeit. Peace is not the opposite of war, any more than death is the opposite of life. The poverty of man's imagination, or the poverty of his inner life has created an ambivalence which is absolutely false. No man can really say that he knows what joy is, until he has experienced peace. And without joy there is no life. Our diseases are our attachments, be they habits, ideologies, ideals, principles, possessions, Gods, cults, religions, or what you please. Good wages can be a disease just as much as bad wages. Leisure can be just as great a disease as work. Whatever we cling to, even if it be hope or fate, can be the disease which carries us off. Surrender is absolute. If you cling even to the tiniest crumb, you nourish the germ which will devour you.

Why didn't you ever go back?

There was the fear that I would never again find the same setting as it was. And don't forget that when I did go back to America, in the space of a year or two I was living in Big Sur—which was an American equivalent of Greece. The wonderful sun, the Pacific, the ocean, you know, everything—forest and quiet—I was alone, . . . solitude, . . . a rare thing.

Once back, resting up and taking stock, it was clear that we had lost sight of our limited goals—that we had been caught up in the Miller stream of consciousness, total recall, and unconsciousness. Overwhelmed by "bills and groans," I tried to interest some investors: After all, this wasn't a pig in a poke, We had hours and hours of footage and the beginnings of a treatment for a documentary feature film! No dice.

But we were careening along Henry's "ovarian trolley" and there was no turning back. We had to go for broke—and we made it.

Frances Inglis, then head of the Fine Arts Productions for UCLA who reigned over the garishly huge Royce Hall and the elegantly small Schoenberg Hall heard of the work in progress and said, "Sight unseen, we'd like to premiere a film of Henry Miller by you. When could you have it done?" "Sometime in the spring." She reviewed her enormous calendar and fixed a date: April 12, 1969. Shortly thereafter she phoned to report that she'd discussed it with the UCLA's Intercampus Cultural Committee, and they'd agreed to sponsor a nine-campus premiere. Now, that's one way of patronizing a project, even "commissioning" it: guarantee its use. "My patrons pay me and I finish the painting," as Michonze says.

Now we started editing—and, intermittantly, filming more and more since Henry went right on living and wanted us to film some of that living. Working our way out of the material, trying day and night to shape the ever growing ungainly amoebic mass.

I began to feel like a fly struggling to get free of sticky molasseslike paper. And Henry's account of his failure to complete his study of D.H. Lawrence became the fixture of continuing nightmares; an embarrassment of riches, a fatal trap. And somehow I felt that this multifaceted, kaleidoscopic chameleon, this Dadaist-surrealist, Emerson-Thoreau-Whitman-Lao-tse Rabelasian deserved the most all-at-onceness insane obscene portrait possible. . . .

I'd come into it one way, and get lost in the labyrinth; start again from another angle, and get stuck in the maze. Meanwhile, I began to be aware of a strange phenomenon: Looking at the footage on the Moviola, a basic piece of editing equipment, I began to be fascinated by the image itself; it was taking over, and everything I had learned by precept, example (from the days when I sat at the feet of Robert Flaherty, the father of the documentary to when I taught the first courses in "film appreciation" myself at various universities and conducted the third largest film society in the United States—in Washington in 1944-1945), and even my own direct experience of "doing," were thrown out the window. Instead of intercutting inserts where he would refer to June/Mona, the family portrait, or the rolltop desk— incidents for which he had provided me with lists of shots on paper or discussed verbally—I can only say that as I looked at, say, the film of Henry in the pool, the hallucination of the image began to take over. I couldn't take my eyes off him. When I would show him rough assemblies at his home, he'd protest: "Christ, you can't hold on me that long in the pool—they'll get waterlogged, they'll get cold. What's happened to the shots of Brooklyn for which I gave you such a detailed list?"

"Henry, I'd rather show the list. Let 'em get cold and waterlogged."

Enter une être étoilique, Anaïs Nin, whom I had the great fortune to meet in the course of the filming. (She had graciously inscribed Diary I: For Bob, equally engaged in portraits of our times . . . wish you'd been there with your camera.") She generously consented to review the various rough cuts of material when I turned to her for help.

Anaïs reassured me that it was all good—but I was trying too hard: Why not start from the beginning and let it flow?

Which is what I did.

And it became clear that "The Brooklyn Years" and "The Paris Years" alone would make a long enough film. Hence, the abrupt "Epilogue" which we "held open" for filming his seventy-seventh birthday celebration, which could be the means of waking him abruptly from his "dream"—a fragmentary account of his picaresque life in Paris. In the course of a wild party, naturally, there is hardly any conversation worth recording . . . there was much good food and drink, good Ping-Pong, some singing and piano-playing (especially an offering by Jakob Gimpel—the concert pianist—) and a lot of horsing around, especially by the old maestro, Henry's take-off of the concert artist . . . in the course of which he composed a damned good dadaist piece.

Birthday party at HM's home

Background singing
Happy birthday to HM;
calls for speech, applause

HM improvising at the piano

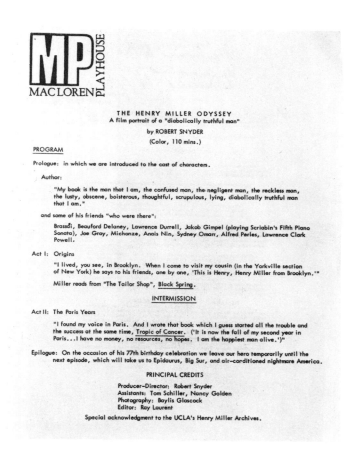

MP MACLOREN PLAYHOUSE

THE HENRY MILLER ODYSSEY
A film portrait of a "diabolically truthful man"
by ROBERT SNYDER
(Color, 110 mins.)

PROGRAM

Prologue: in which we are introduced to the cast of characters.

Author:

"My book is the man that I am, the confused man, the negligent man, the reckless man, the lusty, obscene, boisterous, thoughtful, scrupulous, lying, diabolically truthful man that I am."

and some of his friends "who were there":

Brassaï, Beauford Delaney, Lawrence Durrell, Jakob Gimpel (playing Scriabin's Fifth Piano Sonata), Joe Gray, Michonze, Anais Nin, Sydney Omarr, Alfred Perles, Lawrence Clark Powell.

Act I: Origins

"I lived, you see, in Brooklyn. When I come to visit my cousin (in the Yorkville section of New York) he says to his friends, one by one, 'This is Henry, Henry Miller from Brooklyn.'"

Miller reads from "The Tailor Shop", Black Spring.

INTERMISSION

Act II: The Paris Years

"I found my voice in Paris. And I wrote that book which I guess started all the trouble and the success at the same time, Tropic of Cancer. ('It is now the fall of my second year in Paris...I have no money, no resources, no hopes. I am the happiest man alive.')"

Epilogue: On the occasion of his 77th birthday celebration we leave our hero temporarily until the next episode, which will take us to Epidaurus, Big Sur, and air-conditioned nightmare America.

PRINCIPAL CREDITS

Producer-Director: Robert Snyder
Assistants: Tom Schiller, Nancy Golden
Photography: Baylis Glascock
Editor: Ray Laurent

Special acknowledgment to the UCLA's Henry Miller Archives.

And, if there is an epilogue, there must be a prologue. The "Prologue" served principally to introduce the cast of characters ("and some of his friends who were there").

Lawrence Clark Powell

Joe Gray

Birthday party at H.M.'s house —
"and his friends who were there."

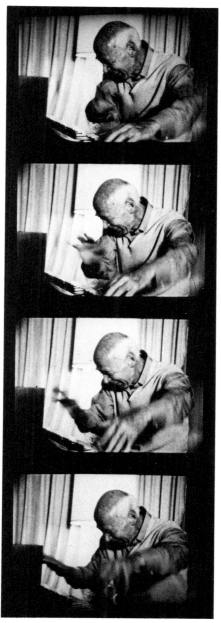

But if the substance of the film was the central character's recollections, it might all be a dream. I had long since observed that Henry, like most geniuses, had the faculty of napping at a moment's notice and sleeping like a baby. Indeed, I had sneaked a few stills of him in bliss. On one occasion, he had played analyst to my bright young apprentice, Tom Schiller, who was complaining of arthritis. So Joe Gray and I set up Tommy to complain about his aches, to lure Henry into giving him another treatment; and if the "treatment" worked, then Tommy was to invite Henry to get on the couch—and that would somehow get us to his first memory and the body of the film would unroll. We had already filmed him in his bathroom, clowning in front of the mirror when he greeted himself for the first time in the morning, and for the last time before going to bed. So here we go:

Picasso for President

Looking intently at an ear, that weird appendage. . . . What is an eye, or a pair of lips, or an ear? Suddenly, you see—that it's not an eye or an ear, but a little universe, composed of the most extraordinary elements. One is astounded by the metamorphosis a human countenance undergoes. Rabelais: 'For all your ills I give you laughter.' To laugh at yourself is the most important thing. Not at others, but yourself—that's the great thing. The day I graduated from high school, we were all asked what would we like to be. I had no idea what I wanted to be so I said, "I think I'm going to be a clown." A symbol of man's suffering on earth, you might say, and of his conquest over it, too. But I was saying a great truth. Because at bottom I think there is a great deal of the clown in me. I'm kind of a schizoid type, who laughs and cries at the same time.

"My book is the man that I am, the confused man, the negligent man, the reckless man; the lusty, obscene, boisterous, thoughtful, scrupulous, lying, diabolically truthful man that I am."

With some of his friends who were there:

Jakob Gimpel, world-renowned pianist and dear friend.
 From the piano): One call . . . and an answer . . . (*hums the theme*) two voices . . . (*and continues playing*).

HM: Mmmm . . . mmm. I know what you mean. Music—you sound a note; that leads to the next note; one thing determines the next thing, do you see. And when you get down to it philosophically, as in Zen, the idea is to live from moment to moment. This move decides the next step. You shouldn't be five steps ahead, only the very next one. If you keep to that you're always alright. But most people are thinking too far ahead, and out into sidelines. Think only what is right there, what is right under your nose to do. It's such a simple thing—that's why people can't do it.

Beauford Delaney, the amazing and invariable Beauford Delaney; the nearest to a saint that any artist can be.

(*Background conversation between them, as they enter BD's garrett studio.*)

AN: You know, I just finished this book about writing and writers; and I said if people would only trust the artist to do the dreaming. . . .
HM: I don't know. God, I don't know.

LCP: Oh, this must be the cast of characters—for what? It's *Capricorn*, the *Capricorn* plan; it's a plan for *Capricorn*. (*Reads*) "Ideas . . . obsessions, descriptive bits; the old neighborhood, Cezanne settings . . . father's shop . . . Styles—

Dissolve to CU of
HM asleep on couch in
his living room

MCU: HM clowning in
front of bathroom
mirror (intercut with
clown watercolors
by HM. Voice over

Dissolve to poster of
full-length photo of HM,
tilt down to main title,
"Robert Snyder presents
THE HENRY MILLER
ODYSSEY"

Piano music background
(Scriabin's Fifth Piano
Sonata) "with some of his
friends who were there---"

Background conversation
HM and Delaney as they enter
Delaney's garret studio

Dissolve to Anaïs Nin and
HM seated in garden

Copy (?) pla[illegible]

DISCUSSIONS

Emma Goldman – Free Love and Anarchism
Nietzsche, Stirner, Kropotkin, Bakunine
Darwinism – Evolution
History of Human Marriage
Bergson – Mysticism – D. F. Mills
Evolution of Idea of God
Sex – Vagaries & Perversions
Karl Marx – Socialism – The I.W.W.
George Bernard Shaw
Religious Cults – Oneida Community, Holy Rollers etc.
Failure & futility of Christianity
Theosophy, Spiritualism, New Thought
The World War – Teutonism
Ethics – attitude toward parents
The glory & validity of Rabelais
Jean Christophe – with Lou Jacobs { Walter Water
Charlie Chaplin & the Movies
Love – { Effects of age, Duration, Constancy
Death and Suicide
Beauty of Scholarship
Negro Culture and History
Walt Whitman & Horace Traubel
Debs, Larkin, Flynn, Tresca etc
Venereal Diseases – Freaks
Christianity vs Atheism { Emma Jones
The Harvard Classics

CHARACTERS

Challacombe
Dewar
Schneider
Einstein
Stanley
Wright
O'Regan
Tom Ogden
Father
Jack Lawton
Tillotson
Berg
Hartman
Tomijero Asai
Frank Reilly
Wardrop
Burger
Grinden
Stone Hill
Charles Trach
Jim Thornton
Poindexter
L'Estrange
Platé
Lou Jacobs
Lionel Allyn
Stockham
Ed. Perry
Urbanski
Hubert Harrison
Archie Morton
Harry Martin
George Wilson
Charlie Sullivan
Baron de Planta
Geo. Kammelkamp
Chas. Baxter
H.W. & Albert Phillips
Fred Chase
Major Carew

Cora Seward
Louise Ashley
Frances Hunter
Helen Sullivan
Edna Booth
Ida Lane
Aunt Emilie
Anna Wagenschutz
Florence Martin
Miss Carpenter
Louise Carmen
Lottie Jacobs
Norma Burger
Mrs. A. C. Burger
Gertrude Imhof
Jennie Main
Lillian Trach

Males – (Cont.)
Baron de Planta
Jimmy Pasta
Benjamin Fry Mills
George Kammelkamp
Karl Karsten
Paul Keals

…lity & religion
…work
…n parents & relatives
…t reformers
…ing Cora
…e on my Love
…ran, Wright, etc
…ence – for[illegible]
…d scholarship
…trary artist
…in books
…ensing – Paul
…t life – Arizona
…physical culture
…suicide mania
…rhood
…nd friends
…philosophy
…life – ugliness
…for both causes
…ing Cora
Pauline

DESCRIPTIVE BITS

The Old Neighborhood – Cezanne settings
Fathers Shop – 5 W. 31 St.
The Wolcott Bar
Emma Goldman's meetings
Free-for-all forum at Madison Square Garden
Tom Sharkey's Saloon
Daily walk from Delancey St. to Shop
The Pre-war Tenderloin district
Six Day Bike Race – Bronco!
A meeting of the Xerxes Society
New Year's Day in Greenpoint
Taking Cora Seward out – violets
French Whorehouse at Herald Square
Getting drunk with Bill Dewar
Philosophizing with Challacombe at Tilford's
Lou Jacobs' home
Holiday feast at Heller's or Smith's
Funeral and feast at Lutheran Cemetery
Visiting Imhofs at Glendale & Bensonhurst
Battery A – Heavy Artillery – Irving Sq. Church
Return to Pauline from California
Affair in gallery at Parsifal performance
Edna Booth in Catskill Mountains
Times Square – open forum – early part of War
Vacations with Henry Dammann – "Weenie"
Taking Aunt Emilie to lunatic asylum
Thoughts on coming first child – abortion – 6 months

STYLES

Dostoievski for Xerxes Society settings
Knut Hamsun for frustration theme – Cora & Pauline
Frank Harris for Frances Hunter & Edna Booth scenes
Tagore for religious vagaries of Challacombe & D. F. Mills
Spengler & Paulsen for philosophic discussions
Anatole France for Lou Jacobs' views on life, love etc
Somerset Maugham for Wolcott & Decatur St. themes
Dos Passos for descriptive bits – gorgeous colors, etc
Ingersoll & Tolstoi for religious disputes
Romain Rolland for idealism, romanticism, etc.
Kropotkin & Sorel for agitators' meetings
Sinclair Lewis for rantings against bourgeois ideas & customs
Dreiser for desertion theme – futility of industry, etc.
Sherwood Anderson for yearnings and introspection

HM: Styles, let's see that one . . .

Dostoyevsky for Xerxes Society . . .

HM: See, see; you get me what a cunning bastard I am—and what shall I say, a cheat? Still I'm thinking what style I can use, not my own, do y'understand.

LCP: (*continues reading*): "Dreiser for desertion theme; Sherwood Anderson for yearnings and introspection."

HM: How do you like that! That hits me, I don't remember all this.

LCP: Henry Miller, for what? What was left?

HM: Yeah, where do I come in?

LCP: You're the coda; the index!

Lawrence Clark Powell and HM outside Powell Library at University of California, Los Angeles; they walk into Special Collections room, examining an early working chart

You know that one of the first things that I remember about you is once I'm standing on the Boulevard Raspail, trying to read French, and there was *vécu*; and I asked you what does that mean, and I learned that it's the past participle of "to live"—it's so simple— I only knew *vivre*.

HM and Gregory Michonze

Of course, in writing, I think, one writes to discover himself. In this thing, I'm just playing—I attach no importance to what I do in painting, not at all. I'm just having a good time. And, I think that this is a very important part of life—that people learn how to play, and that they make life a game, rather than a struggle for goals, don't you know.

Dissolve to MCU: HM at studio table at home, with a water-color of his own in front of him

Lawrence Durrell came to see me in Paris at about the age of twenty-three or four as a young writer, and has remained an ever-lasting friend.

Dissolve to HM and Durrell

Sydney Omarr, a friend of many years standing—now quite famous as an astrologer. . . .

SO: Sometimes we can take the horoscope or the birth data, and tell some remarkable things.

Sydney Omarr and HM in sitting room in HM's home

I have always been very interested in the occult, because I cannot accept this world. I know there is another world behind it which is the real world. The occult embraces many domains, from the gift of prophecy to palmistry and the reading of tarot cards. I've had my palm read and it's unusual that the heart and the head lines run together—they shouldn't. Yet my heart and my head run together. Now, ah, what does it mean? I don't know. I'm as interested in the knowable as in the unknowable, which is infinite.

Alfred Perlès, whom I often refer to as Alf, my boon companion throughout the ten years' stay in Paris, author of a number of books in French, German, and English.

Dissolve to
HM, and
Alfred Perlès

Brassaï, world-famous photographer; for me, the eye of Paris. Also writes, paints, sculpts. . . .

HM with Brassaï in
studio

Joe Gray . . . Joe, ah, this is our third session in this historic film. (*Chuckles.*) It'd better be good. The first one was at your pad, you remember: I posed you as a veteran of the screen. But you had a couple of broads there, and I think they got drunk and ruined it. The second time, you were the ex-pug at the fight manager's place. I think I've got you now in your real role in life. Now, I've always told you that if you hadn't been an actor or a prizefighter, you could have been a great teacher. You come out of like a rabbinical tradition; and you're a bit of a psychiatrist, you're a healer—you like that. Uhh, Dr. Gray, I called you in today because I have a strange case; he's got strange symptoms. For example, he's complaining about arthritis. Well, to begin with, he's only about 20 or 21, a little young to have arthritis all through his body; in another six months, at this rate, he would only be able to crawl on the floor, do you see. I just can't envisage such a situation. Now, I could heal arthritis, or earaches, or something like that, or stuttering, but if a man is love-sick, I don't get very far with him, generally speaking, because I don't like to go back to the womb and all that business. I like to keep within the realm of, what shall I say, of immediate circumstances. . . .

HM with Joe Gray
at HM's desk

HM and Gray at Tommy
Farr's Boxing
Museum.
Back to desk

What is the name again, is it Tom?

TS: Tom, Tom Schiller.

HM: Is that your pseudonym or your real name?

HM with Chinese skull-
cap and Joe Gray
in living room; cut
back to reveal Tom
Schiller on studio
couch

TS: It's my real name.

HM: That's your real name, you were born that way?

TS: Yes.

HM: You weren't baptized?

TS: No, no.

HM: That already tells us something (*Laughter*). Were you circumcized?

TS: Yes.

HM: Tom, don't you think this is a very common thing with young people, this unrequited love on the part of the parents, this lack of affection?

TS: Everybody . . .

HM: It's almost every case today, isn't it? And don't you find, Tom, don't you think that children who think that way are really wrong about their parents? That their parents *do* love them, but perhaps don't show it in the way the child expects?

JG: Were there any other children in the family?

TS: Yes, I have a brother, a younger brother.

JG: Does he get more favor with the parents?

TS: No; now I don't think that's the thing—

HM: Now, listen, young man: First of all, it's not your place to say what you think. We don't want to know what you think—we're the ones who think—(*laugher.*)

JG: We're analyzing *you.*

HM: The moment that he realizes that everything is in his hands, and he doesn't blame his parents or the world or society, he's a long way already to the goal of things. And the main thing now is to assume this responsibility, completely, don't y'know, so that he can say confidently to himself, he doesn't need anybody—I alone can do it, I alone am responsible for everything that happens to me.

JG: In other words, he has to accept the situation.

HM: Don't you think he has to consider that point, when we ask him to

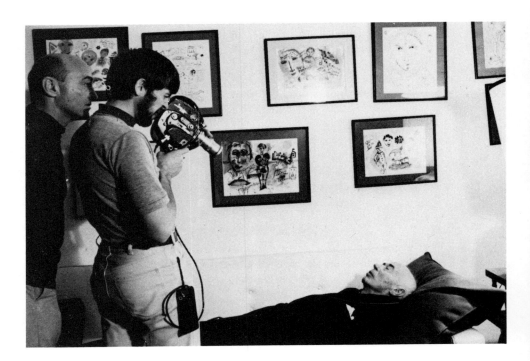

love without being loved? This is a most difficult thing to do. In fact, I, Doctor, with all my wisdom and experience, I don't do it. Tom, as you go about the world, and you meet a man with no problems, come to me, give me his name and address. I want to meet him.

TS: But why don't you get down on the couch?

JG: There's a switch of roles.

HM: You want me to get down there? All right.

HM on couch

JG: The master becomes the patient. . . . (*laughter.*)

HM: Ohhh, I've got real arthritis.

TS: Are you sure that it's real?

HM: Yes, this I'm convinced of. But mine comes about because of age, I think; you know, age and abuse of bodily functions, you know: my stomach gets cramps, my toes curl up and I can't straighten them out, I get insomnia very frequently.

TS: But tell me, for someone who strikes me as having the answers to life, why do you have insomnia?

Dissolve to poolside, HM and Hoki Tokuda, his fiancée; HM's Japanese lesson

HM: I was in love with this girl, this Japanese girl. (To Hoki): If I step on your foot, I'm sorry—(Japanese translation by Hoki). And I have difficulty going to sleep; and then I did these things (watercolors) with her in mind. You see there's a lot of writing on them—they're crazy things, words popped into my head . . . Japanese nightmare style, Scorpio . . . Scorpio was her sign. . . .

Dissolve from watercolors to a woman's face to a photo of HM's mother

All the Hoki-doki chez elle

Les world loves a lover

Une femme où suis-je?

symboles ne mentent pas

Toujours disponible

Happy days are here again

We worked ever more feverishly as the World Premiere approached. Henry took sick at the time—no causal connection; if I had, well, then. . . . So, three weeks before the date, we set up an interlock screening of the penultimate, if not the final, rough cut in his living room—for his approval.

Our whole team arrived to find his inner circle of friends and family (including Anais), all festive except me. I made the usual opening speech, apologetically explaining a "rough cut."

Lights out. . . . Lights on.

Henry, smiling, slowly asks, "Bob, are you sure you won't have to get up on the stage at Royce Hall and make a speech to the effect that owing to conditions beyond our control . . ."

"Henry I promise you, no speeches; if need be, God help me, I'll run it in this condition; but dammit, we'll finish it on time." (Which we did on the morning of the evening. His abiding criticism, after he had seen it a month later—he was still not well enough to make it to the premiere—was, "Mmmm, . . . you have a tendency to dot the i's and cross the t's. It isn't crazy enough." True enough, alas.)

The premiere was a great success; but we never got a commercial release. However, the patient didn't die: the film went out slowly, but surely, to other major university concert series. And then NDR (one of the major German TV networks) asked to audition it; and they telecast a one-hour version. So, malgré Henry's reservations, it won great acclaim.

Envoi: As of this writing, May 23, 1974, we have actually filmed "our hero" up to the celebration of his seventy-seventh birthday, and "we leave him temporarily until the next episode, which will take us to Big Sur, and air-conditioned nightmare America." I don't know when, if ever, we'll be able to put it all together—which I'd do like a shot if . . . if we only had the money.

But if we have it all in the can, dear reader, I feel obliged to give you a few morsels of Milleriana, a bouquet which we can gather under the heading of Picasso for President, one of his favorite games of peopling his ideal republic.

HM: In any great society there ought to be room for those who disagree with the views of society, they should be able to live on the fringe, these people who don't believe. If the society is a great one, what has it to—what has it to fear from a few men who are in

disagreement with it? Why don't you let these men refuse to do all the things that you think are necessary and important? Lead their own lives. What harm can there be to a society? Maybe a great deal of good, Picasso for president, y'know, Casals vice-president, or vice versa; Charlie Chaplin, Secretary of State maybe, and, uh, men like that.

And Dali—Maybe he'd be the jester, the court jester. I think he'd be a marvelous court jester. . . .

And Marcel Duchamp is another man I would appoint to high position—Marcel Duchamp . . . and Hesse and Gandhi.

It should have been an eye-opener for you to read that chapter in The Books in My Life. At various times you've credited me with a live interest in certain writers and thinkers who, to tell the truth, were only passing fancies. My loyalty and admiration, or adoration rather, has been constant for the same men all through my life. Whitman, Emerson, Thoreau, Rabelais above all. I still think no one has had a larger, healthier view of man and his universe than Walt Whitman. And there was always Lao Tse, even before I read him. He stands there at the back of one's head like the great ancestor old Adam Camus—what's all the fuss about, take it easy, sit down, don't get quiet or get quiet, rather, don't think, think—and from him the line of Zen masters which I only got wise to from the Villa Seurat days on—When you walk, walk. When you sit, sit. But don't wobble.

letter to Lawrence Durrell

When I got back to America I had that strange feeling that I ought to see my own country once again and look at it with fresh eyes. I'd been away practically ten years and I wanted to see what America could look like and if I could like it. Because I had left it with no hope of ever returning. It happened that my friend Abraham Rattner, the painter, and I, we bought a cheap car and we decided to make the tour of America. And all this is recorded in the book called the *Air Conditioned Nightmare.*

The publisher's dummy of *Leaves of Grass* served as his notebook on the trip.

Wherever I went, I saw nothing of interest that would hold me, make me want to settle down there; it seemed everything was done the wrong way, you know, with the wrong attitude. And, of course, it's gotten more that way, in my mind. The country really is going to hell in my opinion, don't y'know, is going rapidly. I think many people now see that. Even in the early days of relative calm and prosperity I saw the worm in the apple like; y'know, in this country, . . . the

wrong slant toward life. Materialism, the scientific trend, the importance of the business world, and the domination of that world over everything, the lack of esthetics, do y'see.

Henry, I'll never forget the time of the letter to the *New Republic*, and this stuff began to pour in the . . .

Reading from the New Republic:

From The New Republic Mail Bag

Henry Miller is by common consent of the critics one of the most interesting figures on the American literary scene. He is the author of four books, "Tropic of Cancer," "The Cosmological Eye," "The Wisdom of the Heart" and "The Colossus of Maroussi." His frankness about sex made it necessary for one of his books to be published abroad, and has presumably restricted the circulation of other work of his. He refuses, however, to compromise with what he considers the outrageous prudery of American publishers, although, as he says, "An artist who is non-commercial has about as much chance for survival as a sewer rat. If he remains faithful to his art he compromises in life, by begging and borrowing, by marrying rich or by doing some stultifying work which will bring him a pittance."

Being unable or reluctant to follow any of these courses, Mr. Miller is frequently hard up. We have received from him a communication, unfortunately too long to print, in which he suggests that he will sell some of the water colors which he paints as a hobby, to our readers. "I do not pretend to be a painter," he says. "I do not think my work has any value as art. But I like to paint and I like to think that whatever an artist does by way of avocation is interesting and perhaps revelatory." He adds: "I am putting no price on these paintings if I may call them such. I offer them with the understanding that the buyer may name his own price. . . . I can offer you only what I have on hand at the moment. You will have to take a chance on me." And as a final ironic comment on the life of the uncompromising artist he says: "Anyone wishing to encourage the watercolor mania would do well to send me paper, brushes and tubes, of which I am always in need. I would also be grateful for old clothers, shirts, socks, etc. I am 5 feet 8 inches tall, weigh 150 pounds, 15½ neck, 38 chest, 32 waist, hat and shoes both size 7 to 7½. Love corduroys."

Mr. Miller's address is 1212 North Beverley Glen Boulevard, West Los Angeles 24, California.

Powell

And I looked, went after you, and you said, "My God, they sent me a tuxedo." You were walking up and down like this, holding the

garments, "What'll I do with it?" I said, "Wear it, sometime, some occasion—be ready. When you're called, have your tuxedo on, you may be called anytime." You said, "No, I'll make a scarecrow of it." You took it outside and put it on the picket fence. And it was there for a generation. There it was, the tuxedo scarecrow of Bevery Glen.

HM: I remember the one water-color show where I sold out everything. My first show in Hollywood by the way was . . . some women had a gallery, and I was living in Beverly Glen. This was a period when I was making water colors and you could have them at any price you wanted. A dollar if you wanted, because I needed money, remember, and I'd make you a water color. So finally I got this show and she sold every damn one, yeah. That was just when I came back from Europe.

R.S. Yes. . . .

HM: I wasn't getting any royalties from Europe because the war had cut me off and I had very little in American royalties. New Directions, my publisher, didn't sell many of my books at that time. I was really living at the mercy of my friends. They took me in, kept me. I made two friends who used to come and buy my water colors and buy them like that: I'll take that one, I like that one. I'll take that one. And pay me cash. I always loved to see them reach in, these two men, pull out a fat roll with a rubber band, and do this . . . peel it off, y'know. And they'd say, "How much?" and say "Whatever you say," do y'know. They were very generous with me; I was getting 50 and 75 dollars for a water color, y'know, which was a lot to me. I've always lived very poorly and I don't like luxury, and I don't like having maids. I don't have a maid. In Big Sur I did a lot of housework myself. I swept the floors and washed the dishes and cooked the meals y'know. I don't like to it anymore, but I can do it, y'know. I got embarrassed I had this habit, I did everything myself and I used to cook for friends, have wonderful meals at night and cook in a space you'd never believe. I would say . . . a little cubicle . . . and on a two-burner thing—cook for five or six people. Yeah, but I don't know how to do it anymore.

R.S. That sort of happen after Greece, Henry?

HM: Yes, that was when I came back from Europe—about a year and a half, two years later. I'd been in Hollywood, living there for a year and a half—and then, by accident, I was thrown into Big Sur.

I've never chosen to live anywhere, or just been put there by force of circumstance. I have never deliberately chosen a place—not even Big Sur which was my best place, that was an accident, too.

R.S. In what way?

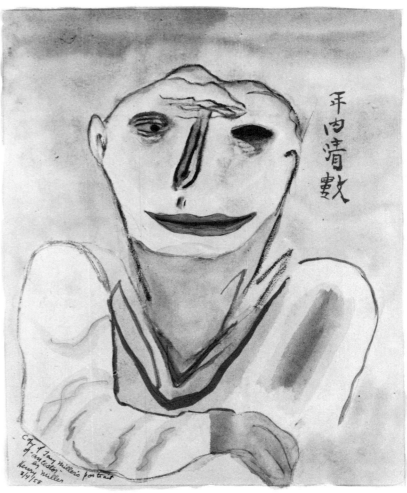

平內清數

Copy of Tony Miller's
portrait of ancestor
Henry Miller
2/4/58

Well, I was invited up to Monterey by that man who does those collages there, Jean Varda, very famous for his collages. I've got three of them in there and there's one right back of you on the wall there, one of his. He's famous for these. He came to see me in Beverly Glen and said why don't I come up sometime to Monterey where he had a barn that he lived in. And after I'd lived with him for ten days he began to be worried that I'd live with him forever; see, he was broke and I was broke. He takes me to Big Sur to visit some friend and suggests I stay overnight. I stayed again two months until this woman found me a cabin up there to live in. That's how that happened, all accidental. In the case of Big Sur, I liked it very much, it was the first place in America I felt at home in. I really found my home there, y'know.

In a way, it was kind of Hamsunish. I mean, your first experience of nature and, probably, it was your first experience in isolation.

Yes, it was . . . it was.

Like Thoreau . . . nature . . . and your interest in Thoreau.

Yes, yes. Of course, there are two kinds of isolation, and in this case I would almost call it a deliberate one, a chosen one, in which I like my isolation, whereas starving in a big city is an isolation that's incredible, you know, that's it. I was a city man; I used to say I couldn't live in the country—it would be dull and stupid and all that, y'know, and then, suddenly, I fell in love with it and with my loneliness and living alone. . . .

Why, actually, did you leave Big Sur?

See, the trouble always is that your good friends—what shall I say—have modesty, and feel for you and they don't come, they keep away. And I could always write my good friends and say, Don't come; if they'd ask me could they come I'd say, y'know, I'm busy. And here the bores come and you can't stop them—that was what was driving me crazy.

Is that really why you left?

No. There were other reasons which I'd say were very personal. I had been divorced, and it was very difficult for me then, a lot of things happened all at once. Oh, yes, the third reason was that my children, who were young then, like twelve and ten . . . they wanted me to come down here, they were living here (Pacific Palisades) with their mother, and they said why don't you come and stay with us. I had already been remarried, Imagine! and I came back and lived with my ex-wife here just for the children's sake. It didn't last very long. That's

how I live in this house; she picked this house, and in a year's time it was all finished and she moved out; the children remained with me.

HM: I always have this feeling of being split. I'm a man of peace, let's say, and I've a great fighting instinct in me, do y'know. I seem to be gentle, but I can be cruel, I know. And I embrace very contradictory ideas, for I can swallow them all and take them into my system—ideas that are opposed to one another.

But no one, it seems to me, can honestly put his finger on the real and vital influences which affected his course. That's why I mentioned, along with books and people, trivial things as well—things, happenings (little events), dreams, reveries, places.

In a book, for example,—I say in a book and not *the* book, or a certain book—there are lines, just lines, page so and so, top left, that stand out like mountain peaks—and they made you what you have become. No one else but you could respond to those lines. They were written *for* you. Just as everything else which happens to you was intended *for* you, and never mistake it. Particularly the bad things.

(And this reminds me to say again that perhaps one reason why I have stressed so much the immoral, the wicked, the ugly, the cruel in my work is because I wanted others to know how valuable these are, how equally if not more important than the good things. Always underneath, you see, this idea of 'acceptance'—which is Whitman's great theme, his contribution.)

I've always lived very poorly and I don't like luxury, and I don't like having maids. I don't have a maid. In Big Sur I did a lot of housework myself. I swept the floors and washed the dishes and cooked the meals y'know. I don't like to do it anymore, but I can do it, y'know. I got embarrassed I had this habit, I did everything myself and I used to cook for friends, have wonderful meals at night and cook in a space you'd never believe. I would say . . . a little cubicle . . . and on a two-burner thing—cook for five or six people. Yeah, but I don't know how to do it anymore.

R.S. You had a lot to say about women—what are your feelings? Do you hate women?

HM: Do I hate women? This is so strange. Not at all. To the contrary. What makes people ask that question sometimes is because I have depicted them pretty brutally and nakedly. I've often restricted love to the sex act—because I know better than anyone that love includes sex—but it's beyond it and better than it. But in writing that book and other books, being truthful and relating only my own life and own experiences, I had to tell what happened to me, and those things weren't pretty—weren't ennobling.

Les Amant Foutus

That's a strange mistake that critics and moralists make, that because an author chooses to write or select or limit what he describes in his book as his experience, that this constitutes his whole experience. As a matter of fact, I have deliberately left out of my work all the other side—that's quite private with me—especially because I've revealed everything. And yet, every man does keep secret and sacred certain things. And I have preferred to reveal the worst side. . . .

R.S. You might be called the founder of the sexual revolution . . . you're the guy who's responsible. . . . What do you make of the revolution that seems to be sweeping the Western world?

HM: Frankly, I don't know what to make of it. It's not exactly the kind of revolution I would want to be excited about. When I was 21 and I heard Emma Goldmann, the anarchist, speak about "free love"— that was the expression then—it sounded good to me. Uh, it was more a question of being able to have sexual relations with the person you were in love with. But today, the way I see it, the word love is sort of omitted. They talk a lot about love-ins and love and love, but I don't feel that the unions between couples are based on a great love for one another. It's more like experimentation. I think this complete freedom doesn't make for something interesting. They're bored very quickly, d'you know.

Letter to Larry Durrell How well I know the tremendous decalage between what one wishes to do and what one does! Nowhere in my work have I come anywhere near to expressing what I meant to express. Now, if you can believe this, and I am sure you must because you must also suffer it, then imagine what sort of beast it is that a woman, any woman, has to live with who marries a writer. Imagine what happens to one who never says all, never does all, who smiles and nods his head in that civilized way and is all the while a raging bull. Well, what happens is that either the writer gains the upper hand eventually, or the man. One or the other must take the lead. My effort has been to give the lead to the man in me. (With what success others know best.) But there is no war involved, you must understand. It is rather a matter of leaning more this way than that, of shifting the emphasis, and so forth.

And I do not want to be a saint! Morality, in fact, drops out of the picture. Maybe the writer will drop out too. Or the man. Never the ego, rest assured. Nor do I give a damn about that.

I certainly do not hope to alter the world. Perhaps I can put it best by saying that I hope to alter my own vision of the world. I want to be more and more myself, ridiculous as that may sound.

Where the writing is concerned, I did nothing consciously. I followed my nose. I blew with every wind. I accepted every influence, good or bad. My intention, was there—as I said, merely to write. Or, *to be a writer*, more justly. Well, I've been it. Now I just want—to be. Remember, I beg you, that this infinitive is 'transitive' in Chinese. And I am nothing if not Chinese.

But this business of youth—rebellion, longing for freedom—and the business of vision are two very cardinal points in my orientation. At sixty-six I am more rebellious than I was at 16. Now I *know* the whole structure must topple, must be razed. Now I am positive that youth is right,—or the child in its innocence. Nothing less will do, will satisfy. The only purpose of knowledge must be certitude, and this certitude must be established through purity, through innocence. Fred can tell you of the unknown man from Pekin who hangs above my doorway here. When I look at him I know he knows and is all that I expect a human being to be. (The photo of him is on the back of the Penguin edition of the Colossus. Study it. That is the person or being I would like to be, if I wanted to be someone else than I am.)

Next day - april 12

For me, painting is playing. . . . To the Chinese all this thinking and creation is just a game. There is no ultimate significance to it, it's just a game. It's the best game there is. But it's only a game. It's a beautiful way to look at it as a game rather than this pious attitude about making us perfect and enjoying our future, that it will be marvelous, and love thy neighbor as thyself—but a game, a great game in which tremendous forces are put at work, against one another—where evil, and justice and right are of the same proportion. They both play a part and nobody can figure it out. This is also another thing that I like that none of us will ever be able to figure this game out, but we can work within this frame work that's been given us to a limited degree and even enjoy it.

And so, if my memory serves me right, here is my genealogical line: Boccaccio, Petronius, Rabelais, Whitman, Emerson, Thoreau, Maeterlinck, Romain Rolland, Plotinus, Heraclitus, Nietzsche, Dostoievski (and other Russian writers of the nineteenth century), the ancient Greek dramatists, the Elizabethan dramatists (excluding Shakespeare), Theodore Dreiser, Knut Hamsun, D.H. Lawrence, James Joyce, Thomas Mann, Élie Faure, Oswald Spengler, Marcel Proust, van Gogh, the Dadaists and Surrealists, Balzac, Lewis Carroll, Nijinsky, Rimbaud, Blaise Cendrars, Jean Giono, Céline, everything I read on Zen Buddhism, everything I read about China, India, Tibet, Arabia, Africa and of course the Bible, the men who wrote it and especially the men who made the King James version, for it was the

language of the Bible rather than its "message" which I got first and which I will never shake off.

AN: Someone wrote me a very amusing letter, from Australia, and said that you had rearranged his molecules. You had changed the direction of the molecules. Which I thought was a wonderful expression. That's being affected, you see, that is a change.

Like a bridge constantly to life; and in every novel, that was the original dream. And that's what fascinated me so much about analysis, and I didn't find that in the Oriental religions.

HM: Now how is it possible to change humanity so we can live in a world that at least has a semblance of sanity? You know. How is it possible? The Hindus can take a long term view and say, Well, what does it matter? It can be accomplished 50 million years from now. What difference does it make?

The world does not change, you change. And how do you change? By different attitudes. Whether you see it from downhill like the frog as Spengler said or up above like the eagle, or still higher like the Gods, do you know what I mean? That's the only difference there is to me. Because otherwise everything is the same.

No matter what you touch and you wish to know about, you end up in a sea of mystery. You see there's no beginning or end, you can go back as far as you want, forward as far as you want, but you never got to it, it's like the essence, isn't that right, it remains. This is the greatest damn thing about the universe. That we can know so much, recognize so much, dissect, do everything, and we can't grasp it. And it's meant to be that way, do y'know. And there's where our reverence should come in. Before everything, the littlest thing as well as the greatest. The tiniest, the horseshit, as well as the angels, do y'know what I mean. It's all mystery. All impenetrable, as it were, right?:

Finis: When Henry saw this photograph, like a death mask, that we sneaked in while he was napping, he exclaimed, "Jesus, you guy will probably be around filming my death." And, of course, we were reminded of Mark Twain's anti-epitaph. Since that had already been done, he captioned it: "the last sleeper of the Middle Ages"; on soberer reflection, he was reminded of St. Thomas' last words, to which he alluded so frequently: "All that I have written now seems so much straw".

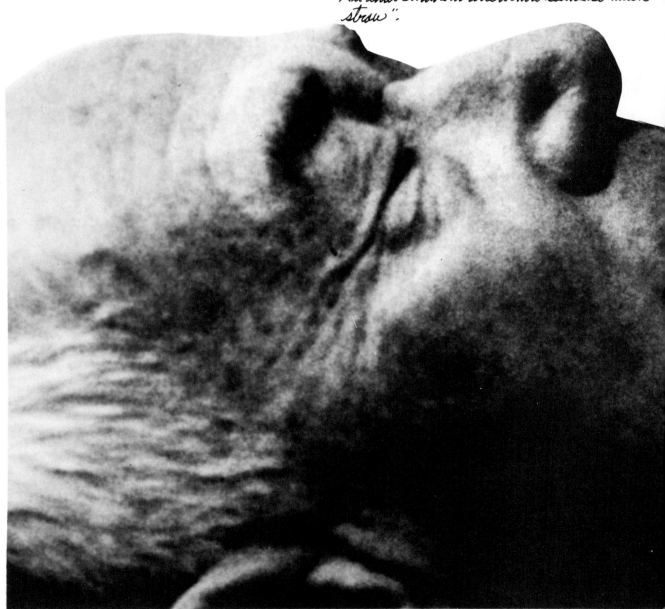

About the Author

Film-maker, teacher, and lecturer, Robert Snyder has had a distinguished and pioneering career documenting the greats in the creative and performing arts, of which Henry Miller is the most recent. Of a twenty-four-minute "fragments of an interrupted conversation with the American author," telecast by the BBC from the filmed memoirs Snyder amassed, the London *Times* reviewer was moved to write:

":. . strangely comforting as evidence that civilized values are still somewhere cherished . . . that someone is still fighting a dogged rearguard action in defense of art."

In so doing, Snyder's films have garnered many awards, starting with an Academy Award for Best Documentary Feature in 1950 for *The Titan: The Story of Michelangelo;* and followed by a Diploma of Merit from the Edinburgh Film Festival for *Visit with Pablo Casals;* Special Award, Best Folkloric Documentary, Bilbao, and the Ciné Golden Eagle for *Bayanihan Philippine Dance Company;* and the most coveted Gran Premio Bergamo for *The Hidden World.*

Born in Manhattan and educated in the east (at CCNY and Columbia —where his MA thesis was on John Milton's Imagery of Light), he resides in Pacific Palisades in California with his wife and two children. His wife, Allegra Fuller Snyder, is on the Dance Faculty at UCLA and Snyder himself lectures periodically on the art of film at various branches of the University of California Extension. He is a member of the Directors Guild of America and Academy of Motion Pictures Arts and Sciences.

Among his magazine-of-the-arts-on-film are: *Sketchbook No. 1: Three Americans* (Buckminster Fuller, Igor Stravinsky, Willem de Kooning); *Vivaldi of Venice* (Part I); *Caresse Crosby: Patroness of the Arts.* Works in progress include *Sketchbook on Pop Art* and a full-length portrait of Buckminster Fuller. His most recent film is *Anaïs Observed: A Portrait of a Woman as Artist.*

But—
Pages
slightly
out of
order!

cut out some of the "ya know"s. !!"
conversation ought to be
edited! (Impossible now — no time!)

Excuse
me!

Hm

Did you pay Grove Press
for quotation from Black
Spring about the roll-top desk?
why change from "I" to "he"
after desk quote (Knut Hamsun)
Pay Grove ~~too~~. for Tante Melia quote?

(There are
a number
of
repetitions

beginning p. 11 — is repetition of
previous page.
paragraph
Cut ~~part~~ about 1918-68

mistake!

Be sure to put quotes around
dialogues!
are you translating French
passages?
There are more quotes —
but you don't say where from!

The text for this book
was set in ten point Palatino by Chris Davis Graphics
on a Compugraphic Compuwriter II;
the display type, Broadway, by Andresen Typographics.
Calligraphy for margin notes was executed by Thomas Warkentin.
The book was edited by Ruth Glushanok
and designed by Kadi Karist Tint.